The Herbal Tea Garden

Planning, Planting, Harvesting & Brewing

The Herbal Tea Garden

Planning, Planting, Harvesting & Brewing

Marietta Marshall Marcin

STOREY
BOOKS
Schoolhouse Road
Pownal, Vermont 05261

The mission of Storey Communications is to serve our customers by publishing practical information that encourages personal independence in harmony with the environment.

For my father and mother ⎯⎯⎯⎯⎯⎯⎯⎯⎯⎯⎯⎯⎯⎯⎯⎯⎯⎯

Published by Storey Communications, Inc., Schoolhouse Road, Pownal, Vermont 05261. Originally published in 1983 by Congdon & Weed, Inc., as *The Complete Book of Herbal Teas*. Developed and produced by Roundtable Press, Inc.

Text copyright © 1993 Marietta Marshall Marcin

Edited by Sandra Webb
Cover design and production by Meredith Maker
Cover photograph © 1992 A. Blake Gardner
Illustrations © 1983 Ray Skibinski
Text design by Betty Binns Graphics
Text production by Michelle Arabia

Printed in the United States by Book Press
10 9 8 7

The Herbal Tea Garden is not intended as medical advice. Its intention is solely educational and informational. Please consult a medical or health professional should the need for one be warranted.

The information in this book is true and complete to the best of our knowledge. All recommendations are made without guarantee on the part of the author, Roundtable Press, Inc., or Storey Communications, Inc. The author and publisher disclaim any liability in connection with the use of this information. For additional information please contact Storey Communications, Inc., Schoolhouse Road, Pownal, Vermont 05261.

Storey Books are available for special premium and promotional uses and for customized editions. For further information, please call the Custom Publishing Department at 1-800-793-9396.

Library of Congress Cataloging-in-Publication Data

Marcin, Marietta Marshall, 1932–
    The herbal tea garden : planning, planting, harvesting & brewing / Marietta Marshall Marcin.
      p.   cm.
    Rev. ed. of: The complete book of herbal teas. c1983.
    "A Garden Way Publishing book."
    Includes bibliographical references and index.
    ISBN 0-88266-827-7 (pbk.)
    1. Herbal teas.   2. Herbs.   I. Marcin, Marietta Marshall, 1932–
Complete book of herbal teas.   II. Title.
    TX415.M37   1992
    641.3'372—dc20   92-54653
                                             CIP

CONTENTS

Acknowledgments

THANKS to the following, who gave generously of their time and expertise to help make this book possible:

In Great Britain, to Guy Cooper, Co-Director, The Herb Society, London; Elspeth Napier, Editor, *The Garden*, Journal of the Royal Horticultural Society and M. V. Mathew, Librarian, Royal Botanic Garden, Edinburgh.

In Canada, to Ina Vrugtmun, Librarian, Royal Botanical Gardens, Hamilton, Ontario.

In Australia, to Alan M. Gray, Education and Information Officer, The Royal Tasmanian Botanical Gardens, Hobart; D. Conderlag, Librarian, Mt. Coot-tha Botanic Gardens, Brisbane; Helen M. Cohn, Librarian, Royal Botanic Gardens and National Herbarium, Victoria; Marni Morrow, Herbalist, Clarence Gardens, South Australia; and Pauline Moss, Meadow Herbs, Mount Barker, South Australia.

In the United States, I was helped tremendously by Dr. Rupert Barneby, Botanist, New York Botanical Gardens, and Dr. Michael Nee, Botanist, Field Museum of Natural History, Chicago, who examined the manuscript and illustrations.

Aiding me in my research were librarians Virginia Henrichs of the Chicago Botanic Garden and Horticultural Society; Michele Calhoun, of Field Museum of Natural History; Mary Alonzi of Winnetka Public Library; Georgine Olson of the Lake Forest Public Library, and Marietta Marcin II, who sent me much valuable information.

Pertinent data about the herbal tea market was provided by Mark Blumenthal of The American Botanical Council and Robert McCaleb of the Herb Research Foundation.

Others who helped make it possible for me to finish the manuscript on time were: Jack Garrity and Sue Lenard, who gave from their gardens so I could experiment more fully with tea blends; Jayne Ames; Dr. Stephen Graham; Phebe Waterman; Toby Chamberlain; Amy Greenstadt; Janet Steinberg; Tom and Sheila Masloski; James R. Nash; Richard Nash Jr.; Frank Nash; and Nancy Iran Phillips, who worked on deadline to photograph me in my herb garden before fall frosts could snatch away its beauty.

Special thanks to Karl E. Meyer for his help and encouragement, and to Susan E. Meyer and Marsha Melnick of Roundtable Press, who gave me continuous support during the many months between my initial plans for the book and its completion.

Introduction

A FEW years ago some pesky mint appeared in my garden and began to spread, crowding out carefully cultivated annuals and perennials. I was beginning to plan a massive eradication program, when I came across a recipe for mint tea. Well, I thought, why not try it? The raw ingredients certainly were available. So I pulled up a few handfuls of mint and brewed my first cup of home-grown tea. It tasted great. So great, in fact, that the endangered garden mint took on new significance and was spared. The following year I planted lemon balm, fennel, marjoram and thyme, and tried those recipes, too. The result? I became hooked on herbal teas.

Later, I learned tea is drunk more than any other liquid except water. Throughout recorded history tea has been used to sustain life, enhance sleep, restore health, and ease conversation, to name just a few of its uses. Some people like it hot. Some like it cold. Some like it mixed with sugar, lemon, honey, milk, or with stronger stuff, such as gin or brandy. And some like it straight.

In the narrowest sense of the word, tea refers to the leaves or flower buds of shrubs in the genus that was named *Thea sinensis* by Swedish botanist Carolus Linnaeus. Since *Thea sinensis* tea is a close relative of the camellia flower, it is sometimes referred to as *Camellia thea* or *Camellia sinensis*. Broadly speaking, however, tea is any drink made from steeping fragrant leaves, berries, seeds, flowers, roots, or bark in boiling water.

Imported *Thea sinensis* teas all come from evergreen plants of the same genus. Lapsang souchong tea is a smoked version of *Thea sinensis* leaves, and black, green, and oolong teas can also be made from leaves of the same plant. They differ only in the degree of fermentation they have undergone during processing. Most imported teas are grown at high altitudes where it is continually hot, wet, and very humid. Darjeeling tea, for example, comes from the mountains of Darjeeling, in India.

Imported *Thea sinensis* teas traditionally have been served side by side with teas made from herbal leaves plucked from the garden. Indeed, the decision to serve *Thea sinensis* teas rather than herbal teas has often been made more for reasons of prestige than for taste.

As coffee prices have gone sky-high, so too has the price of store-bought teas escalated. But as I found, you can easily grow and brew exotic herbal teas, full of tastes and aromas you never believed possible. The cost to you is a few pennies a cup; the experience is priceless. Herbs that make exciting teas can be grown in your garden or in flowerpots on your windowsill, whether you live in southern California or northern Nova Scotia.

This book gives you all the information you need to brew the perfect cup of herbal tea. It spells out how to grow the plants, harvest the tea components, prepare and store the ingredients you'll need, and mix them for interesting blends. You'll learn where to buy seeds and plants. You'll even find where to buy bags and containers in which to package your own "private label" blends. Sound complicated? It's really easy once you know how. And, while you're harvesting herbal teas either on a small or grand scale, you can also use them as potpourris, fabric dyes, garnishes, and seasonings for the cooking pot.

People have always sworn by the medicinal qualities of herbal teas. While the Food and Drug Administration frowns upon claims that herbal teas can actually cure ailments, millions of people maintain they do. I'll outline some of the medicinal uses to which herbal teas have been put. But by no means are the herbal teas described in this book presented as prescriptions for medical ailments. Clearly, as with any medical problem you may have, it's important to consult a professional practitioner for diagnosis and treatment.

This book is the only guide you'll need to take the journey of taste discovery that comes from brewing herbal teas. Let us take that trip together.

1. A brief history of tea

EEP in the misty mountains of China, the Bodhidharma, the founder of Zen Buddhism, sat in a garden near the emperor's palace, meditating on the perfection of Buddha. Called Ta'Mo' (White Buddha) by the Chinese, the swarthy, rotund saint had come to China from India bearing the sacred bowl of his ancestors. Ta'Mo' vowed to demonstrate his devotion to Buddha by sitting before a wall and meditating for nine years.

Spring turned to summer; autumn came with crisp air and colored, falling leaves. Still Ta'Mo' meditated. Winter came and covered the saint's cloak with snow as he sat unblinking and unsleeping. Finally, after many years had passed, the Bodhidharma's attention wavered, his chin dropped, and his eyes closed in sleep.

When Ta'Mo' awakened—perhaps a day, perhaps a year later—he was so angry with himself for neglecting his meditation that he took out a knife, sliced off both his eyelids, and threw them to the ground. The saint's eyelids took root in the rich soil and grew into a tea bush, the symbol of wakefulness.

This is the most popular of the legends about the origin of *Thea sinensis*, the botanical name for what is commonly called the tea plant, which we associate with black, green, oolong, and orange pekoe teas. Like other stories about the origin of tea and the rituals of tea drinking, fact and fiction are intertwined so thoroughly that it is hard to separate them.

The discovery of Thea sinensis *tea*

Ta'Mo' died about 530 A.D., but the Chinese claim they discovered the tea plant much earlier. They called it "the gift of heaven," and it was mentioned, along with other herbs used for medicinal purposes, about 2737 B.C. in the writings of the legendary emperor Shen Nung.

According to legend, Shen Nung observed that people who boiled their drinking water remained healthier than those who didn't, so he always made sure his water was boiled. On a trip to a neighboring province, the emperor's servants started a fire to boil water for him. As the water was heating, a breeze blew some of the tender leaves from the uppermost twigs of the firewood into the pot. Attracted by the fragrance of the resulting liquid, the emperor "tasted it and found it good," as the saying goes. Thus began a tea-drinking custom that has persisted to this day.

Originally the tea made by infusing the *Thea sinensis* herb was used only as a medicinal brew, as were teas made from many other herbal plants. *Thea sinensis* tea soon became a popular beverage because of its flavor, and the word *tea* came to be associated with this plant. Although the cultivation of tea began in China, it gradually spread to Japan and the rest of the Far East. It was not cultivated in India until 1832, when the British introduced it there, long after it had become a popular beverage in England and the United States.

Derivation of the word tea

The word *tea* has an interesting history. When *Thea sinensis* tea was first introduced in England it was pronounced *cha* or *tcha* from the Mandarin and Cantonese dialects spoken in Macao, the port from which the tea was shipped. When a Cockney housewife says it would be nice to have "a cup of char," she is speaking perfectly respectable Chinese, a holdover from the original word. Later tea was imported to England from the Chinese port of Amoy. In the Amoy dialect, it was called *t'e*, and it was from this word that the word *tea* was derived.

The word *tisane* came from the Latin *ptisana* and the Greek *ptisane*. Originally, tisane meant pearl barley and barley water, but over the years it has come to mean any infusion of herbal leaves in boiling water.

Tea comes to England

No one knows for sure exactly when *Thea sinensis* tea was first brought to England, but in 1658, an enterprising merchant named Thomas Garway placed an advertisement in the publication *Mercurius Politicus* announcing that: "The excellent and by all Physitians approved China Drink, called by the Chineans Tcha, by other nations Tay, alias Tee, can be procured at Sultaness Head Cophee-House in Sweeting's Rents by the Royal Exchange." Garway extolled the medicinal qualities of tea as a stimulant. He wrote that "tea removeth lassitude, vanquisheth heavy dreams, easeth the frame, and strengtheneth the memory. It overcometh superfluous sleep, and prevents sleepiness in general, so that without trouble whole nights may be passed in study."

Dutch ships from the Orient brought tea, along with other "riches of the rising sun" to Holland, and from there Lords Ossory and Arlington began bringing consignments of tea to England. What started as an infant trade quickly became a rage. Soon *Thea sinensis* teas were being served in all of England's most famous coffeehouses.

As the popularity of tea drinking grew, tax revenues from the sale of beer and wine declined. To compensate for this loss of income, in 1660 Charles II imposed the first English tea taxes, paving the way for a thriving black market in tea.

The earliest American settlers did not share the English passion for drinking imported teas. Tea drinking was probably introduced to the colonies somewhat later, by the burghers of New Amsterdam. William Penn brought *Thea sinensis* tea to the Quaker colony he founded in what is now Delaware in 1682. But by the 1750s, American colonists were quaffing tea as heartily as the English.

Early recorded uses of herbal teas

Herbal teas, other than *Thea sinensis*, have been brewed for thousands of years. The earliest records talk of using herbs for healing rather than flavoring. In 410 B.C., Plato mentioned herbal teas in his writings. Seventy years later, Aristotle discussed herbal teas, and his disciple Theophrastus wrote a detailed work, "On the History of Plants," which described the uses of herbs. Herbals with detailed illustrations, and instructions for brewing herbal teas, have been revised and expanded ever since.

The Roman statesmen Cicero, Seneca, and Pliny the Elder practiced advanced forms of horticulture and wrote about their experiences. Pliny's *Natural History* (77 A.D.), affirms the importance of growing herbaceous plants both for kitchen and medicinal uses. He outlined how to plant, transplant, and harvest them. Pliny also spelled out the medicinal uses of each herb, as well as how to administer each one—as lotion, powder, or tea. Many herbal teas were to be brewed with water and vinegar, he said, which may explain why herb teas weren't popular as beverages until later, when they came to be brewed in water alone. His descriptions of the juices and flavors of each herb characterize savory and wild marjoram as having "an acrid taste," others as being "sweet" or "pungent."

Pliny catalogued the germination times of many herbs, noting that some plants continued to appear every year, while others had to be newly sown from seed if they were to come up again. "No seed is more prolific than basil," he said. "They recommend sowing it with curses and imprecations to make it come up more abundantly."

Wealthy Romans took their herb culture seriously. The mild Italian winters still were not quite warm enough to keep some tender herbs from being destroyed, so plants were placed under thin sheets of mica (plate glass had not been developed yet) to protect them from the chill. And warm water was often piped around the roses, which were particularly admired for both their beauty and medicinal qualities.

Herbal teas in the New World

In England, herbal teas were widely cultivated and used. When the Pilgrim fathers sailed to the New World, they brought seeds or plants of their favorite herbs with them. Most larger houses had both an herb garden and a "still room" for cultivating herbs.

While the tea of *Thea sinensis* remained the favorite herbal beverage, those who couldn't afford it continued to make teas from other, more easily accessible herbs. Chamomile, peppermint, and elderflower teas were especially popular.

One herbal tea beloved of the colonists was Oswego tea, made from the dry flowerheads of American wild bergamot (*Monarda didyma*), also called bee balm. (The resulting liquid tastes like one of the scented Chinese teas.) Some say the colonists learned to make Oswego tea from the Indians, others that it was devised as a New World version of a European tisane.

After the Boston Tea Party, patriotic ladies banished imported tea—termed "the baneful herb" by the clergyman and educator John Andrews—from their tables and turned to domestically grown herbal teas. They called these beverages "liberty teas." Some of their herbal combinations—made from mint, balm, rosemary, and sage—are still favorites today.

After the Revolutionary War, the Americans imported tea directly from China, and *Thea sinensis* became easily attainable and inexpensive once again. A few of the more flavorful herbal beverages were still used, but most home-grown teas were returned to the medicine chest. Imported herbs were now also easy to come by, for those who wanted them, so the cultivation of herbs declined, too.

It wasn't until the outbreak of World War I that England and America were faced with the unpleasant realization that they had become largely dependent on German sources for medicinal and cooking herbs. There ensued an upsurge in home-grown herb cultivation.

Recent growth in the herbal tea market

In the past, the use of herbs in cooking was never as great in England and America as it was in the rest of Europe and, particularly, France. About 20 years ago, however, many Americans began moving away from a steady diet of meat and potatoes cooking towards ethnic and gourmet cuisine, which meant there was an increased use of herbs in the kitchen.

The natural foods movement also contributed to a growing appreciation of herbs and their health sustaining qualities—they have no additives, artificial coloring, chemically produced flavors, or caffeine.

An outgrowth of America's increasing interest in gourmet cookery and organic and natural foods was a slow but steady increase in the consumption of herbal teas. Herbal tea drinking was given an additional boost by wide publicity about caffeine's being not only an artificial mental and physical stimulant, but also an addictive substance. Coffee, cocoa, and *Thea sinensis* teas contain caffeine; herbal teas do not.

Ten years ago, when packaged herbal teas were accounting for 60 percent of the European tea market, they comprised only 10 percent of the United States tea market, up from virtually nothing a few years earlier.

Twenty plus years ago, the industry leader, Celestial Seasonings, Inc., wasn't even in business. By 1975, five years after it began marketing colorful little boxes of herbal teas through health food stores, the company broke the $1 million mark in sales. Sales doubled in 1976, and by 1981, gross revenues had risen to over $23 million.

Along about that time, Lipton and Bigelow, sensing a sharp inroad into the China tea market, jumped onto the herbal tea bandwagon. Today, Celestial is still the largest producer of herbal teas.

It's estimated that the combined gross sales of herbal teas by Celestial, Lipton, and Bigelow alone now run around $200 million yearly, and are continuing to grow.

Herbal teas are now widely offered in restaurants, and are universally available wherever groceries, health foods, and organic foods are sold.

Retail sales of herbal products for food, beverage, and health purposes in the United States have also leaped from between $300 to $400 million a year about 12 years ago, to $1.2 billion annually. According to the American Herbal Products Association, this is, necessarily, an estimated figure, and doesn't include sales of herbs for potpourris, environmental products, culinary purposes (spices and herbs in foodstuffs), and the floral market. Estimates of the size of this increasing market (including herbal teas) is probably low, because herbal products packagers are often small, privately held companies whose sales figures are not released. They may distribute at retail, through mail order, or directly.

The Food and Drug Administration entered the herbal tea picture several years ago, ordering two companies to stop producing sassafras tea, an age-old prescription for upset stomach and for nerves. When boiled, sassafras releases a substance called safrole, a known carcinogen which the FDA has banned as a food additive. Researchers later discovered a person would have to ingest more sassafras tea in a day than most people do in a year in order to get the same concentration of safrole that had produced some cancers in laboratory animals. There is no doubt, however, that excessive use of certain herbal teas can be injurious to your health.

The U.S. Department of Agriculture's Medicinal Plant Resources Laboratory created a stir several years ago when Dr. James Duke warned that catnip tea could be hallucinogenic if taken in excess. It was also announced that bloodroot tea can be toxic and possibly carcinogenic. This herb contains some of the same alkaloids as opium, and, despite its bitter taste, was used as a narcotic by Native Americans.

Despite these gloom-and-doom announcements, however, most herbal teas are beneficial, not poisonous, if drunk in moderation.

One of the most highly touted herbal teas is ginseng. Tour any herb store or Chinese emporium and you will see a hefty display of it. Ginseng is believed to increase sexual potency, lengthen lifespan, and produce a feeling of well-being. Korean red root ginseng,

Korean white root ginseng, Manchurian ginseng, Manchurian red ginseng, Canadian ginseng, and, for the connoisseur, Imperial Chinese ginseng, are considered the finest ginseng teas available. They are thought so potent that they are usually taken only once or twice a year. One variety of ginseng, *Panax quinquefolium*, is increasingly grown in the United States although it is difficult to cultivate.

The FDA concerned itself with ginseng for a while, but doesn't anymore. FDA laboratory tests indicated ginseng has no effect on the body whatsoever, though satisfied ginseng users beg to differ.

Producing enough herbs to meet the new demand for herbal teas has become something of a problem. Since they must be picked by hand, most herbs are grown in Third World countries where labor costs are low. Many herbs are also picked wild, or are purchased from small growers with backyard plots, though an increasing number are being cultivated both in the U.S. and abroad, now that a demand for them has mushroomed.

Controlling quality by growing your own herbs

Harvesting, processing, and shipping delicate herbs grown in many different places can make quality control difficult. You can surmount these problems though, by growing herbs yourself. You won't be growing them in such great quantities that pickers will be hard to find. You can sort and prepare them, keeping their quality as refined as your taste. And you can experiment with blending them, augmenting the blends with a few ingredients from your local herb supply store, if you wish.

Herbs you grow for tea also make good additions to salads, soups, or main dishes. Extras can be used in potpourris, sachets, herbal butters, and vinegars, or to make decorative, long-lasting floral displays that scent your home long after the growing season is past.

People with vegetable gardens—and it is estimated that more than one-half of all families in the United States now grow some of their own food—find herbs are easy to grow. In fact, mint, bergamot, chamomile, and dandelion have been growing around us, wild, all along. So let's move on to the practical business of growing these herbs, and many others, and discovering just how easy it is to brew your own herbal tea delights.

2. Guide to cultivating herbs

THE most pungent herbs are said to grow on rocky hills near the Mediterranean coast. There, in poor, dry soil where the sun beats down on them all day, a high concentration of essential oils (which are what give herbs their flavor and aroma) builds up in the leaves. This is nature's way of keeping the plants from drying out and dying. Early growers tried to duplicate the austere environment of these native plants. They believed poor soil, little water, and hot sun would guarantee the most aromatic basil, thyme, and rosemary. No matter that they had to harvest half an acre of plants for a few handfuls of leaves; the taste and aroma made it all worthwhile.

Today's herb gardener has neither the space nor patience to grow stunted, small-leaved plants that yield one teapot's worth of herbs when the garden is stripped. Fortunately, plant geneticists have developed herbal strains that have large amounts of essential oils in their leaves but are also big and bushy plants that thrive in good, well-drained soil.

The indoor gardener, using improved seeds and plants, as well as modern growing methods, can get a fine yield of herbal tea from a single potted plant placed on a windowsill or under grow-lights. The outdoor gardener can derive immense satisfaction and a gratifying crop from a small herb plot tucked in a sunny corner or on a small patch of ground near the kitchen door.

Whether you're starting your herbs from seed, nursery plants, or cuttings or rootings given to you by generous friends, you'll want to ensure their success by providing them with a good growing environment.

Preparing the soil

Most of today's herbal strains do nicely in aerated soil that is well drained, crumbly, and enriched with a moderate amount of fertilizer or organic matter to supply the plants with nutrients.

To check how good your soil is, insert a spading fork to its full depth. If it goes in easily with little or no effort, you're lucky—you probably already have ideal soil for your herbal teas. If it scrapes or won't go in all the way, you'll have to do some work. Usually, this will mean adding conditioners. Most soils benefit from the addition to their bulk of up to ⅓ peat moss, compost, sawdust, or leaf mold, well mixed, to a depth of at least 1 foot. If you have clay soil, you'll want to add even more of these conditioners to get an herb planting bed that will provide good drainage and enough friability so the root systems will remain moist (but not soggy) and will spread easily.

If you have impossibly heavy clay soil or an impermeable layer of hardpan not too far below your planting surface, you can create a raised planting bed filled with a more desirable soil mix. Raised beds can be surrounded by bricks, railroad ties, rocks, boards—anything sturdy enough to keep the earth contained. Incidentally, a raised bed not only guarantees good drainage but also becomes warm and dry earlier in the spring, allowing you to plant sooner than at ground level. For this reason, many gardeners whose soil is good still prefer raised planting beds for their herbs.

Avoid preparing your soil on a day when the earth is wet and sticky and will compact. You can test for the right time to cultivate by taking a handful of earth and squeezing it together into a ball. Press this lump gently with a finger of your other hand. If it holds together, the ground is too wet to work. If it crumbles, it's time to roll up your sleeves and start digging.

Be sure to distribute soil conditioners evenly throughout the mixture. Start by spading your bed to the depth of the spading fork, so that it's loose. Then spread the organic materials over the surface and systematically dig them in. As you insert your spading fork, turn the soil to one side or the other so that the organic materials trickle through the tines of the fork and down the face of the soil the full depth of the spade. This way you avoid leaving the soil on top of organic matter that is buried in a layer underneath.

You may work the soil several times before it is the right consistency, but once you've paid your gardening dues by creating a good planting bed, it can be maintained easily for several years and will reward you with bigger, healthier plants.

Checking soil acidity and alkalinity

After you've worked conditioners into the planting area, you should check the pH factor—acidity or alkalinity—of the soil. The pH scale runs from 0 at the acid end to 14 at the alkaline end. Most herbs do well in a fairly neutral pH range of 6.0 to 7.5.

For a nominal fee, your state agricultural extension service will analyze a sample of soil to determine the pH factor. Or you can test it yourself with the type of kit sold at any garden center.

If you find the planting mixture is too acid, mix 5 pounds of agricultural limestone into each 100 square feet of planting area to raise the pH by ½ to 1 point. If the mixture is too alkaline, add 3 pounds of iron sulfate or aluminum sulfate to each 100 square feet to lower the pH by ½ to 1 point. For the few herbs that prefer more acid or alkaline concentrations, you can spot work these minerals into the soil around the plant.

Planning for outdoor planting

If you're planting seeds outdoors, plan carefully where you want to put them (see chapter 3 for full information on planning your garden). By planting right where the plants will be growing, you'll know exactly which herbs are where (but it's still a good idea to use label markers to help jog your memory). Also, you can thin the herbs in place; and you won't risk loss from later transplanting.

Water your planting area well the day before you plan to seed. This way, newly sown seeds will get the necessary moisture to help them sprout, and there will be less likelihood of washing them out just after they've been planted. Make sure all danger of frost is past and that the soil has begun to warm up. If there is a short growing season in your area, slow-growing plants with long germination periods should be planted earlier, indoors or in a cold frame, then transplanted into the garden when they're established. Otherwise, they won't yield a crop of any significance before the end of the growing season.

For centuries gardeners have considered moon phases when planting seeds, because of the extra light, darkness, and/or gravitational pull provided by the lunar cycle. Generally, it's believed annual herbs (which live one season only) should be planted during the first ☽ or second ○ lunar phase. Biennial herbs (which live two seasons), should be planted during the third ☾ or fourth ● lunar phase. Perennials (which may live many years) should be planted during the third lunar phase. However, all root crop herbs should be planted during the third and fourth phases, when added darkness helps them send their roots deep into the ground. More exact planting time can be determined by consulting your local paper (the weather report usually shows moon phases), or "The Old Farmer's Almanac."

Presoaking seeds

Many herb seeds are slow to germinate but sprout more quickly if you soak them in water before you plant them. The night before I'm going to plant indoors or outdoors, I put seeds of each herb into separate saucers filled with water. I place the seed packet under each saucer, so I'll know which is which when morning comes. Then I lock up my cats, so they won't help themselves to a nocturnal drink from the saucers or mix up the seeds. In the morning, I remove excess moisture from each saucer with a sponge and the tip of a paper napkin. Then I plant my seed varieties one by one.

Planting seeds outdoors

If winters aren't too severe in your climate, you can plant dill, borage, and other slow-germinating seeds outdoors in the fall. They'll come up nicely in spring. Fall planting should be done before autumn frosts begin, but late enough in the season so that seedlings won't emerge before winter only to be killed when cold weather arrives. Check seed packets for average germination periods and for instructions on planting in your climate.

Before you plant, make shallow scratch lines with a hoe or trowel to guide you when sowing. Place seeds in the furrows, and cover them lightly with soil. Seed packets usually spell out how deep seeds should be placed—this varies from herb to herb. If planting depth isn't spelled out, a good rule of thumb is to plant seeds to a depth of two to three times the diameter of the seed.

Make sure the soil covering the seeds isn't lumpy or heavy. You can sift it over the seeds through a screen, making sure it is even and fine.

After you've covered the seeds, firm the planting area with your hand or a board. If the surface has dried out, moisten it lightly with a fine spray of water, being careful not to uncover or dislodge the seeds. In the days that follow, continue to keep the soil damp (not soggy) by watering with a very fine spray.

Many herbs are look-alikes as seedlings. Some, like oregano and marjoram, continue to look like one another even into maturity. Don't count on your memory to remember which herb is which or you might be in for some unpleasant taste surprises when you brew the herbal teas. Label seed rows or planting spots with plastic or wooden markers, using a waterproof, indelible pen. I use 1-inch-square stakes about a foot long, which I drive into the ground 6 inches deep so they won't be uprooted. Each stake is prominently marked with a wide-tipped pen. If markers become dirty and hard to read after a couple of years, I pull them out one by one, sand them lightly, and relabel them.

Annuals and biennials usually germinate more quickly than perennials, but some biennial herbs (like parsley) take a long time to appear. Be patient. If you're using good new seed, have planted properly, and haven't had an excessively cold or rainy spell, the little plants will probably emerge just as you're giving up hope. Remember, though, most herbs germinate best at 70° F (21° C) or warmer, and they prefer 60° to 65° F (15° to 18° C) temperatures once they've sprouted, which is not easy to accomplish outdoors. That's why many gardeners prefer to start seeds indoors under more manageable conditions.

Thinning seedlings

Whether you're planting outdoors or indoors, thin the seedlings after two pairs of true leaves develop, so the remaining plants will have enough room to develop. Try to snip or pinch off weaker seedlings (pulling them up can sometimes uproot good ones), even if it means transplanting strong ones that have sprouted in one area.

In hot weather areas, leave plants closer together so foliage will shade the soil. If necessary, you can thin again when the seedlings are larger.

By all means, save the little plants you've gleaned when thinning. If leaves are the part of the herb used to brew tea, treat yourself to a cup as a reward for your efforts!

Planting seeds indoors

Less hardy herbs, or those that take a long time to germinate, can get a head start if you plant them indoors 6 to 9 weeks before the last frost is expected.

You can plant in ceramic, plastic, or peat pots, or in wooden or plastic flats. All planting containers must have holes in the bottom to provide good drainage, and must be scrubbed absolutely clean so they won't transmit disease to new seedlings via plant pests still lingering from previous plantings. Wooden flats, in particular, may continue to harbor disease-causing organisms. I sterilize mine by putting them into a 160° to 180° F (71° to 82° C) oven for about half an hour. The stench is awful as they're "cooking," but the results are good.

Once they've cooled, fill your planting containers with a good sterile potting mix. You can buy this ready-made, or, if you prefer, you can make your own. One commercial herb gardener who grows thousands of plants each year asserts that gardeners who make their own herbal planting mix will get good results by combining 1 part each of soil, sand, peat moss, and perlite. This mixture is good for both indoor and outdoor herb planting.

No matter what planting mix you decide to use, screen it through a ¼-inch mesh screen (hardware cloth) to break up the particles.

If you're using garden soil and compost, you'll want to make sure the mix is sterile. Bake it in a 160° to 180° F (71° to 82° C) oven for about 2 hours. Once again, the smell will be strong. Plants potted in such soil are unlikely to get damping-off disease, a fungus which attacks seeds and tiny seedlings.

If you want to prevent damping-off disease without sterilization, you can saturate the planting mix with a solution of commercially prepared fungicide. You can also make your own fungicide by mixing 2 parts of finely ground copper sulphate with 11 parts of fresh ammonium carbonate. Store the mix in an airtight glass jar. When you need a solution, dissolve ⅔ ounce of the mixture in a little hot water. Then add enough cold water to make 1 gallon. Store the solution in a plastic or porcelain container (not a metal one) and use it immediately.

Organic gardeners, who shy away from chemical additives, maintain that they can control damping-off disease by:

1. Using sterile potting mixture
2. Providing seed flats with proper drainage
3. Keeping flats in a place that is low in humidity and has good ventilation
4. Sowing the seeds in a mixture of equal parts of compost and sand, and covering the seeds with pulverized, heated clay
5. Sowing seeds sparsely, so they aren't crowded

Once you've filled your planting container with potting soil, tamp it down gently to ½ inch below the top of the flat or pot and water it well.

If you're sowing several rows of herbs in a flat, make shallow indentations about 2 inches apart for each row. I use a pencil length pressed into the mix. Sow seeds in the rows, labeling each row with a wooden or plastic marker, and cover the seeds lightly with sifted planting mix. If the seeds show when you water or mist them, it means you haven't covered them deeply enough, and should sift a little more soil over them.

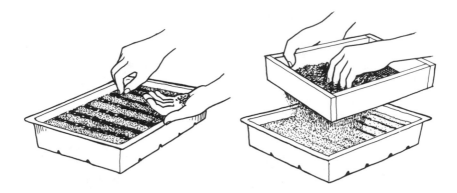

The best way to water newly sown seeds without disturbing them is to place the planting containers in a tray of water. Allow them to soak until you see that the top surface is thoroughly wet.

Annual, biennial, or tender perennial herbs that originated in hot climates usually germinate better if the seeds are kept fairly warm. You can accomplish this by putting an electric heat tape (available at garden supply stores) on the bottom of the flat and keeping it plugged in until the plants have emerged. Or you can place an incandescent lamp under the flat to warm the bottom, keeping the temperature at 70° to 75° F (21° to 24° C).

Providing adequate light

The best place to put flats or pots is in a sunny south window where they'll get heat and light all day. If your window doesn't face due south, you'll have to rotate the flats and pots to keep the plants growing straight.

If you don't have a southern exposure, you can use fluorescent grow-lights. The usual arrangement is two tubes, 24 or 48 inches long, in a commercial shop-type fixture. Mine are suspended from heating pipes in my basement by chains attached with S hooks at the fixture end. This way I can raise or lower the lights to accommodate growing plants. I plug the fixtures into automatic timers, allowing from 12 to 16 hours of light per day.

Regular fluorescent lights can also be used, but they lack some of the benefits of grow-lights, which are designed to promote plant growth. Some gardeners who have sunny windows use grow-lights as well to ensure a longer day for their plants.

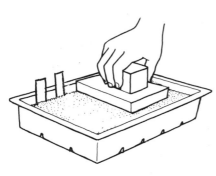

Carefully sow seeds in rows in a flat prepared with a good soil mix, and be sure to label each row or flat so you can identify seedlings when they appear. Next, cover seeds with finely sifted soil only as deeply as recommended, so they won't expend all their energy trying to reach the surface of the soil. Work the topsoil into the corners with your fingers. Finally, lightly tamp down the soil surface after seeds are planted, making sure it is level.

Begin by placing newly seeded flats and pots only 3 or 4 inches under the fixture so emerging seedlings won't become "leggy" trying to reach the light. Once the plants have established a couple of sets of leaves and are doing nicely, you can move the lamps up, or the plants down, depending on your arrangement. Make sure the plants never touch the lights.

If the herbs are in a dry place, mist them daily, but be sure you do this early in the day so they dry thoroughly before the lights go off or the sun goes down. Otherwise, they may develop fungus disease.

But, you say, why should this be? After all, dew forms on outdoor plants at night, and they don't get mildewed. That's true. But outdoor plants have constant ventilation, which can't be duplicated in indoor growing situations.

Be sure to thin indoor seedlings, just as you do outdoor ones.

Transplanting

Seedlings grown indoors in flats or pots, plants raised in the nursery, or cuttings or rootings taken from other plants should all be transplanted carefully if they're to make a successful transition to the hostile outdoor environment with its variations of temperature, wind, and moisture.

To prevent transplant shock, you can "harden" indoor plants by introducing them gradually to the harsh world outside. A few days before the transplanting, place them outside in a warm, sunny, and protected spot. Leave them for a few hours each day, but be sure to bring them safely indoors if the sun stops shining, the temperature begins falling, or whenever wind or cooler weather threatens. After a few days of hardening, your plants should be acclimated and ready for outdoor planting.

Transplant on a mild, overcast day or just before sunset, when the sun will not beat on the relocated plants. The dark and dew of night helps them recover before morning.

If you must transplant on a sunny day, be sure to protect the transplants from excess heat and light by constructing a cheesecloth umbrella suspended on stakes, or by pushing a shingle, floor tile, or leafy twig into the soil on the south side of the plants to shelter them.

To move seedlings, lift them out of their growing containers one by one. Pry up the root system of each with a plant marker, tongue depressor, or spoon, trying to keep as big a ball of soil around the roots as you can. Steady each little herb plant as you move it by gently holding a leaf (not the tender stem, which can easily snap) and lower the root ball into a prepared moist hole. If you've planted in peat pots, you can place each seedling in its hole, pot and all. Expanding roots will grow through the disintegrating pot.

Firm the soil and make a little saucer-like depression around each seedling to catch and hold moisture. Try to set plants no deeper than they were when growing indoors. If, however, they have become "leggier" than you would like, set them a little deeper so they can support themselves without falling over.

Seedlings can be transplanted when they are about 2 inches tall, and have two pairs of true leaves above the rounded pair of seed leaves. Pry up the root ball with a teaspoon or with the pointed end of a plant marker. Hold the herb lightly by one of the rounded seed leaves as you lift it out of the ground. Be sure to replant seedlings immediately after digging them up.

When transplanting herbs, tap the pot until you feel the root ball and earth come loose. If roots are entangled in the drainage holes, work them free (if the pot is plastic, you may cut it apart to avoid damaging them). Invert the pot, holding one hand over the top with your fingers surrounding the herb. When it falls free from the pot, gently transfer it to its new location. Try to keep the pot soil in place around the roots.

Keep transplanted seedlings well watered, making sure you don't uncover the roots or knock them over with too heavy a spray.

Incidentally, you can use this same method if you decide to transplant seedlings indoors because your plants are too crowded, or are coming up all in one spot and not in another.

If you're transplanting nursery plants, try to transfer all the planting mixture surrounding the roots to the transplant hole without disturbing the plant. Tap the pot sharply to loosen dirt from the edges, or if the plant is in a plastic compartment, squeeze the compartment gently to dislodge the mass of soil surrounding the roots. This is easier to do if you do not water plants just before you transplant them. If the soil around them is too moist, it's likely to crumble when you try to remove the plant from its container. If it's drier, it will usually stick to the plant roots and come out in one mass.

If soil does fall off the roots, or if the growing mixture hasn't adhered to the roots, spread the roots in the planting hole gently so they're not in one clumped mass. Then carefully firm soil around the plants and water them well.

Larger nursery plants, rootings, or cuttings don't need quite as much protection from the sun after transplanting as do tiny seedlings, but it's best to transplant on a calm, overcast day or late in the afternoon.

Whenever you're moving plants, be sure the transplant hole is good-sized, so you can surround the newly planted herb with plenty of loosened, prepared soil. And work up the soil in the bottom of the hole to give the roots a soft cushion to rest on.

If soil in the transplant hole isn't the right mix, dig a much larger hole—one big enough to hold the root system of the herb when it reaches maturity. Then replace the soil that was in the hole with the proper planting mix.

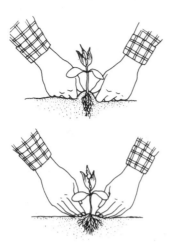

Herb seedlings or transplants should be planted deeply enough so that all roots are covered with soil. The picture at the top illustrates the wrong way to transplant. The roots are being squeezed into a tight ball, and some of them will be uncovered by rain or watering. The picture at the bottom illustrates the correct way. All roots have plenty of room to spread, and the soil is gently firmed around the plant with all roots covered by soil.

When transplanting, don't rely on memory to tell you where you put each plant. Many herbs change appearance considerably as they mature, so it's important to label your transplants just as you would seeds, at least until you've been growing herbs for so many years that you're thoroughly familiar with all stages of their development.

Watering tips

You'll want, of course, to give special attention to the watering of seedlings, nursery plants, cuttings, or root divisions just after you've transplanted them. But there are other general watering tips to bear in mind.

When planning your garden, group herbs that require lots of water in one spot so that they can be sprinkled or soaked at the same time. The herbs that require less moisture should be clustered together to avoid overwatering them when you're tending the rest of your garden.

Herbs like thorough and deep waterings, rather than frequent shallow ones which don't penetrate to the bottom of the root ball.

Mulching

You can cut down on watering if you spread 1 or 2 inches of mulch around your herbs, tapering off to about ½ inch near the stems.

Ever since Ruth Stout advocated heavy mulching in her book,

How to Have a Green Thumb Without an Aching Back, mulching has been regarded as a new phenomenon. Actually, it is a natural process, millions of years old. As leaves fall to the forest floor, they protect smaller plants during severe weather, and as they decompose, they form soil-enriching compost.

Whether it occurs naturally or through the efforts of a conscientious gardener, mulching accomplishes many things. It conserves water by cutting down on evaporation, and it helps keep plant leaves clean when there are heavy rains. This is particularly important in the case of creeping thyme, parsley, oregano, anise, and other herbs that grow close to the ground and are often blown over in heavy storms and pushed into the soil.

Mulching also eliminates weeds and preserves delicate herb feeder roots that would otherwise be destroyed by hoeing or digging. The few weeds that creep through the mulch can be pulled out easily by hand.

Mulching also helps guard against extreme weather by insulating herbal roots from the cold. If the mulch is organic, it gradually decomposes into the earth's top layer, boosting soil fertility by providing helpful microorganisms.

Perennials growing in severe climates benefit from heavier mulching at the end of the growing season, which protects them from extreme cold winter temperatures and keeps their root systems from drying out.

Popular mulches for the herb garden include freshly cut grass, chopped hay or straw, chopped seaweed, cocoa hulls, wood chips, and pine needles. (Grass should be piled on in many thin layers, rather than all at once, to prevent rotting, which attracts insects.) Most gardeners have favorite mulches, depending on personal preference and availability. One caution: If you're mulching heavily for a long period of time, check the pH factor occasionally. Some mulches cause soil acidity—a "no-no" for most herbs. You can adjust for this by adding minerals to deacidify the soil.

Fertilizing herbs

Generally speaking, herbs don't need much fertilizing—they draw their nutrients from the soil they're planted in. Too much fertilizer can cause excess leaf growth, resulting in smaller concentrations of the flavorful essential oils that distinguish herbs.

Commercial herb growers rely on one small dose of fertilizer for seedlings—usually fish emulsion or liquid seaweed. One grower finds that using skim milk instead of water promotes healthy growth in young seedlings.

Most herbs can do without fertilizer if they are mulched with organic matter and if compost is added to the soil periodically. Indoor plants, which don't benefit from these natural fertilizers, thrive with an application of very weak fish emulsion about once every 2 weeks during watering.

Combating pests and diseases

Most herbs are naturally resistant to insects, so much so that they are often companion-planted with vegetables and flowers in order to repel harmful pests. The closer the herb variety is to its original type, the better it withstands insect attacks or disease.

Aphids sometimes attack chamomile and dill, but not excessively. Basil is occasionally stripped of its leaves by Japanese beetles. Generally speaking, though, plant pests tend to shy away from the aromatic herbs.

If pests do become a problem, you should avoid chemical pesticides especially since *you* will be ingesting the teas made from the leaves, roots, flowers, or seeds.

Insects can be eliminated by hand-picking them off plants. Or you can spray your herbs with an insecticidal soap such as Safer's Insecticidal Soap. Approved for use on food plants by the Environmental Protection Agency, insecticidal soap is completely biodegradable, leaves no harmful residue, and can be applied up to the day of harvest. It is made from naturally occurring fats and oils found in the cells of all living things. When sprayed on infested plants, it eradicates from 86 to 100 percent of the most destructive garden pests, but does not harm beneficial insects such as bees and ladybugs. It has a pleasant smell and actually cleans the plants' leaves.

Propagating herbs

Herbs may be propagated in many ways—by seeds, stem cuttings, root cuttings, layering, mound layering, root division, and runners. Different herb varieties are more easily propagated by one method than by another.

Seed propagation

Many herbs, including annual, biennial, and perennial varieties, can be reproduced easily from seeds (sources for seeds and plants are listed at the back of this book). If you have patience and a willingness to work, seeds are by far the most economical way to develop your herbal tea garden. A packet of seeds, usually enough for up to 100 plants, costs little.

As I explained earlier in this chapter, seeds can be planted directly outdoors, or indoors in flats or pots for permanent transplanting to the garden once the danger of frost has passed.

If you're gathering your own seeds from plants you or friends have grown, snip off the seedheads into a paper bag. If the seeds are dry and fine, shake them from their pods and plant them immediately; or store them in a clean, dry place, wait a few days or months, and plant them so they'll emerge at a time you would prefer.

A few herb seeds—sarsaparilla, for example—should be planted immediately upon ripening in order to achieve maximum germination. However, because this plant is much easier to propagate by root cuttings, most gardeners don't bother with seeds. Some herbs are difficult to cultivate from seeds, but self-sow readily. It is easier to transplant the seedlings from these herbs in spring or fall. (There is more detail on individual herbs in chapter 7.)

Lavender, lemon thyme, tarragon, and most mints can be grown from seeds but seldom are, because other propagation methods are easier.

Stem cuttings

Rosemary, oregano, winter savory, lemon verbena, hyssop, lavender, the thymes, and scented geraniums are usually propagated by stem cuttings, because seed propagation of these varieties is painstaking and uncertain.

To reproduce by cuttings, cut off 3- to 6-inch plant tips from healthy, well-established plants during the active growing season. Don't take soft or forced growth, weak shoots from the center of the plant, or vigorous growth from thick stems. The ideal cutting stem will snap when bent sharply, rather than bending without breaking.

Cut each stem sharply and cleanly just below a leaf bud, using a razor blade, sharp knife, or shears (a scissors pinches the stem end, impeding root formation). Make sure the cut is clean, straight across

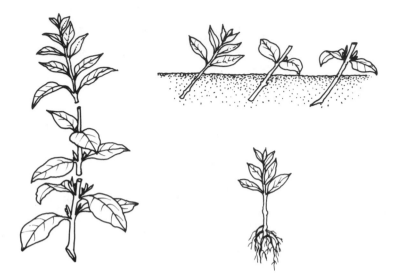

Two or three 3- to 6-inch cuttings can be obtained from one healthy stem. Strip off the leaves from the bottom third or half of each cutting, dip the cutting in rooting powder (optional), and insert it into the cutting mix. Many gardeners believe they get better results if the cuttings are planted at a 45° angle.

or on a slight angle. Gardeners disagree as to which method is more effective, but both seem to work. Make your own choice.

Strip leaves off the bottom third or half of each cutting, and dip the stem into a hormone rooting powder to ¼ inch above the last stripped leaf bud. This step is optional, but the hormone powder hastens root formation. It's available at most garden centers.

Tap off excess powder before you insert the cutting into a hole made in advance in moistened rooting medium. Make sure this hole is wide enough so the hormone powder won't be scraped off when you insert the cutting. Then firm the medium around the cutting to avoid air pockets.

An ideal planting mixture for cuttings is moist sand, or perlite placed in a flat or other container which will provide good drainage. Soil, peat moss, and vermiculite are not usually used in cutting mixtures because without them drainage is better and there is less possibility of fungus. One experienced herb grower swears by a well-packed mixture of 1 part sand and 1 part perlite.

Once you've placed the stems in the cutting mixture, do not allow them to become dry or wilted. Mist the cuttings each morning (never at night) until roots have formed. Some gardeners place a plastic bag over the cutting container to ensure that stems will remain moist. Unless the plastic is removed regularly to admit fresh air, however, there's a danger that molds will form.

Set the cutting container in a place where it will get good *indirect* light—not direct sunlight. Turn the container regularly so that the cuttings will get equal light on all sides.

Lemon balm and thyme will probably form roots in 4 to 6 weeks, but herbs with woodier stems (rosemary, tarragon, and lavender) may take several months.

You'll know roots have formed when the foliage takes on a brighter green color, or when you tug gently on cuttings and discover they tug back. Wait several weeks before trying the tug test, so as not to disturb cuttings unnecessarily. There probably won't be any new leaf formation just after roots have formed, but the cuttings will nevertheless be ready for transplanting into 3- to 4-inch-diameter pots. When transplanting, try to keep as much of the propagating mix around the roots as you can. Again, keep the transplanted herbs moist and out of direct sunlight until new growth is evident.

Three to 5 weeks after you've transplanted, when the plants are 3 to 4 inches high, pinch off the top center of the young herbs to encourage bushing out.

Your plants should be developing nicely come spring. Hardy sage can actually be put outside a month before the last spring frost date, once you've hardened the plants. But wait until after the last frost date to put out tender plants such as bay and rosemary.

One advantage of growing new plants from cuttings is that you know the resulting plants will be true to the old ones. Cutting is an asexual process, while seeds develop through a sexual process and may not look exactly like the plant you took them from. Another advantage of propagation by cutting is that you can get a tremendous variety of perennial herbs quickly this way if you have friends who are willing to let you snip away in their gardens. However, out of deference to your friends' generosity, take cuttings only from well-established plants, ones with several stems and side shoots, not from one-stemmed plants that have been tenderly nurtured indoors all winter and are still struggling to survive outside.

Root cuttings

Some plants—such as bee balm (bergamot), horehound, catnip, and savory—send up new stems from spreading roots. Cuttings from these can create new plants. Select roots ³⁄₁₆ to ³⁄₈ inch in diameter from a well-established, vigorously growing plant. Discard the tapering ends of the root, and cut the remainder into 1- to 3-inch lengths, so that each piece includes some of the fleshy root and a bud. Dust the root pieces with hormone rooting powder, and lay them 2 inches apart horizontally in a flat prepared with the same type of soil mixture you used for stem cuttings. Cover them with about ½ inch of additional cutting mixture, and water the flat thoroughly. Then cover the container with a piece of glass or newspaper, place it in a shady place, and keep the cuttings moist. Remove the covering when leaves appear. Once growth is established, transplant each cutting into a small pot. If leaf growth is heavy, remove most of it before replanting, allowing only one or two small center leaves to remain. Plant each cutting into its pot so that the leaves are above the soil, and the piece of root is below.

The best time to propagate this way is in the spring, when new growth is under way, though root cuttings may be taken any time from spring to fall if you can keep the newly planted roots shaded and moist.

In cool regions, you can take root cuttings in fall and store the cutting container on a sheltered porch or in a cold frame outdoors. Be sure to keep the container well watered. In spring the cuttings will send up shoots and can be planted in the garden.

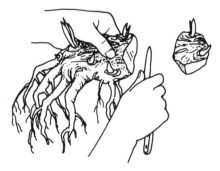

To make root cuttings, dig up the donor plant, and slice sections from the root system. If you want to keep the donor plant, as well as the cuttings, don't slice very large sections.

Simple layering can produce new herb plants. After partly slitting the stem, lay it in a prepared hole adjacent to the donor plant, and tack it down to prevent it from working itself loose from the soil. In time, new roots will form on the buried section. When a good root system has established itself, the new plant can be cut from the donor plant and transplanted.

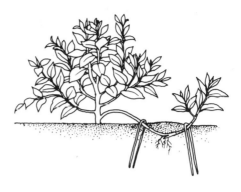

Layering

Layering is often easier than making cuttings. Many herbs, such as sage and tarragon, will layer themselves outdoors when a stem falls over, touches the ground, and sends down roots.

You can layer perennials yourself if you want extra plants. Choose a healthy stem or branch near the ground, one that will bend down easily to touch the soil. Look for a leaf node about 1 foot from the stem tip, and make a small slanting cut just below the leaf node, cutting about halfway through the stem or branch. You can also scrape away the outer layer of bark from a short section of stem or branch without cutting into it and dust the cut or stripped section with hormone rooting powder. This "wounding" method is better for thin stems.

Figure out where the cut or stripped section will touch the soil, and dig a shallow depression there. Mix the soil you remove from this hole with equal parts of peat moss, ground bark, or sand, and put some of this mixture in the bottom of the hole. Then bend the cut or stripped branch down into the hole, anchoring it in place with a heavy wire loop or staple. Pieces of coat hanger do nicely, or for thinner stems, large hairpins will do the trick. Be sure the metal pinning goes deep enough into the soil to hold the layered branch firmly.

Mound the depression with the previously prepared soil, and firm it well. Water and then add a thin mulch of leaves or compost. If you're preparing good-sized branches for layering, you may place a brick or stone on top of the mound temporarily so that the treated portion cannot become dislodged.

Roots usually form in about 6 weeks. Check them by carefully removing the soil and tugging on the stem or branch. If roots are well established, you can sever the stem or branch from the parent plant and transplant your new herb.

If you're layering in the spring, use growth from the previous year. If you're propagating by layering in midsummer, use new growth rather than the previous year's older wood. Summer growth is usually easier to layer because it's more pliable.

You can continue to propagate by layering until 4 weeks before the first frost. Plants that are processed in late summer or fall should be left in place until the following spring, then severed from their parent plant and transplanted.

Mound layering

Mound layering is another way to layer bushy perennial herbs, especially if they branch out from a tight root base. In early fall, pile earth up around the plant, burying the center branches completely to a height of 4 or 5 inches. Make sure the branches are kept covered with moist earth.

When you dig up the plant in late spring, you'll find that roots have formed all over the buried branches. Cut each leafed branch below the new root formation and—presto—instant new plant!

Root division

Perennial herbs with root systems that spread each year and send up new growth are a constant source of new plants. These roots become complete new herbs when they're divided from the parent plant. Angelica, bee balm (bergamot), catnip, oregano, coltsfoot, thyme, and many other herbs are easy to propagate in this fashion once a parent

Mound layering takes time, but it can be a good source of new herb plants. Mound soil around the donor plant, burying center branches, and keep the soil in place until new roots appear on the covered branches. These rooted branches—which are really new plants—can be cut off and transplanted. Be patient when mound layering; don't dig up the plant until good root systems have formed on the buried branches.

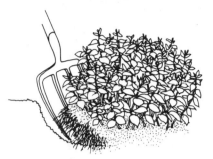

Many plants can be made from one bushy donor. Dig up the plant and split it (as shown), making sure each clump has a good root system. Or, you can slice down around the plant and lift new ones, without digging up the donor. Be sure to fill the resulting hole, and water the donor plant well.

plant has become established and started to spread. Single stem herbs (dandelion and parsley, for example) cannot be propagated this way.

If an herb is spreading beyond where you want it to go, you can create new plants and thin the old one at the same time. Plant propagators suggest gently digging up the old plant and washing the root ball so you can clearly see the spreading roots. Then pull the plant apart or cut off the younger plant growth that has formed around the outside. Discard the older, woodier central growth. Parts you pull off from around the core can be transplanted into water-filled holes prepared with good soil. Surround the transplants with firmed earth to prevent air pockets. Trim some leaves and stems off the new plants to avoid excessive loss of moisture while they reestablish themselves, and if the roots are long and bushy, trim them to encourage new growth. Once planted, the herbs should be well watered until the plants have recovered.

If you don't want to disturb the parent plant, but lots of new growth has formed around the core, drive a spade straight down into a portion of the new growth and separate it from the parent plant. Fill the

35

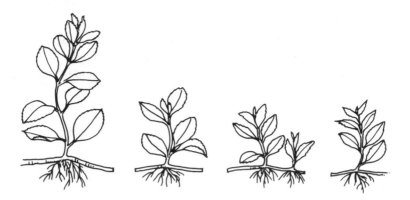

Transplanting herb runners is easy once they already have established a root system. Just cut the runner between each shoot, and transplant the new rooted plants.

hole you created by removing the spreading root section, tamp it, and water the parent plant well. The section you separate from the parent plant can then be processed just as if you had dug up the parent plant.

Root divisions can be made in the spring, before new growth has become so established that leaf damage caused by handling the plant will affect its appearance during the growing season. Or divisions can be made in the fall; new growth the following spring will ensure a compact, attractive resurgence of undamaged herbal leaves.

Runners

Some herbs (such as strawberries) send out runners from the parent plant. Long stems develop, with leaves and root nodes along the way or at the ends. When the runners eventually touch ground, they send down new roots. While these root systems are being established, runner plants continue to take nourishment from the parent plant. Once the rooted plants are coming along nicely, the stems that "ran" them to their new location will wither away.

If you wish to propagate this type of herb, it's easy to help nature a little. You can direct runners where you want new plants, then anchor them into nicely prepared soil to hasten root development. Leave the running stems attached to the parent plant until new plants are established, then trim them off.

In all forms of propagation, a few basic rules apply. The soil bed for propagated plants should be prepared carefully and the soil should be kept moist until new plants have established themselves. Of course, all plant parts involved in the propagation process should be handled gently and watched carefully until the new plants are well developed.

With practice, you can become highly skilled at all methods of propagation. What may sound complicated becomes second nature once you have repeated it step by step a few times.

3. Planning your garden, outdoors and in

O NE of the most delightful things about herbal tea gardens is the way they reflect the idiosyncracies of their owners.

Disorganized gardeners tuck one herb here, another there, yet still manage to enjoy a refreshing cup of herbal tea, when they can remember where they put the plant.

Scientific gardeners carefully plant their herbs next to treasured flowers or vegetables, precisely matching the herbs' insect-repelling capacities with the susceptibilities of other plants, so that each flower or vegetable is protected from its predators.

Fastidious gardeners delight in formal, geometrically correct herb gardens, each plant trimmed to perfection and exactingly placed. A crisis ensues when, to provide tea for unexpected guests, a branch must be trimmed more than planned.

Artistic gardeners arrange plants with aesthetic considerations in mind, whimsically shifting them around each year to create interesting new arrangements.

Besides offering a bountiful harvest, herbs allow you to express yourself. And unlike flowers and vegetables, herbs provide more than just a few short days of pleasure—they provide tea all year long.

Planning the outdoor garden

As you plan your garden, you may want to emphasize color patterns— gray-green sage with its purplish flowers placed near the white or yellow blossoms of feathery yellow-green fennel. You may prefer to plant for a balance of aromas—delicate lavender far from pungent basil; rosemary, with its woodsy smell, close to woodruff, which yields up a forest-like odor after it has flowered and dried. Or you may want to emphasize textures—lace-like, serrated leaves of tansy placed close to the smooth, regular leaves of bay. The creative possibilities are countless.

Before you begin planting, however, consider these basic guidelines to reduce the chance of failure and to get more interesting results:

1. Group herbs that need a lot of water so they can be watered all at one time. Conversely, group those needing little water, so you can spare them when you're sprinkling.

2. If you have several types of soil in different areas of your garden, try to match the needs of the herbs to the soil conditions. This will help cut down on the amount of care you'll need to give them.

3. Make sure all herbs are easy to reach so you can tend and harvest them without trouble. Keep the beds narrow, or create paths through wide beds, so you can gain access to the herbs from behind.

4. Place herbs that thrive in direct sunlight in an area of the garden that gets sunlight all day. Herbs that like full or partial shade should be in an area that loses direct sunlight after the sun passes behind a tree or building.

5. Consider the seasonal patterns of the sun's rays in your planting area, then plant low-growing herbs in front, facing the sun, medium-sized ones behind them, and the tallest in the back. This way all plants get the maximum available sunlight.

6. Plant for color and texture—a patch of blue-flowered herbs in one area, yellow bloomers in another. Or you can soften and emphasize the outlines of stark, single-spiked plants by placing expansive bushy ones nearby.

7. If possible, plant perennials in one area, biennials and annuals in another so as not to disturb the roots of permanently sited plants when you're planting herbs that last only one or two seasons.

8. Plant herbs that tend to spread in areas where they won't smother slower-growing, delicate varieties. If space is limited, you can keep spreaders from going wild by sinking wooden or plastic barriers below ground to contain the roots.

9. Consider the best use or uses for each herb. Creepers can be used as ground cover or perhaps in a rock garden. Tall and bushy herbs can be used as a windbreak for more delicate herbs, or as a hedge or visual barrier. Evergreens can soften the harshness of a building or, if close to a bird feeder, provide refuge for birds during cold weather.

10. Finally, consider the overall ambience of your herb garden. Try to visualize how it will look throughout the growing season, including blooming patterns and bare spots created by early harvesting. Think about how to get more than one crop in a season. Make a continual analysis of the appearance and usefulness of the plants in relation to their growth patterns.

Remember, the most attractive herbal tea garden is not created instantly, but through careful planning for the future, when well-established perennial plants will give it a natural and decorative appearance.

When plotting your garden, consult the compendium of herbs and the quick reference chart in this book. They capsulize basic information on each of the seventy herbs popularly used for tea, and will help you with the placement of herbs in your garden. The compendium also provides information on size and spacing of plants; it is important to allow sufficient breathing room for plants to mature and develop properly.

Here are some of the properties of herbal tea plants that you'll want to consider:

HERBAL TEAS THAT GROW IN SHADE OR PARTIAL SHADE: Agrimony, angelica, cicely, comfrey, dandelion, elder, ginseng, hop, hyssop, Labrador tea, lemon balm, mints (not catnip), mugwort, parsley, pennyroyal, sarsaparilla, sassafras, speedwell, tarragon, valerian, wintergreen, woodruff.

HERBAL TEAS THAT GROW IN MOIST PLACES: Angelica, bergamot (bee balm), coltsfoot, comfrey, elder, flax, hibiscus, hop, jasmine, Labrador tea, meadowsweet, mints (not catnip), mugwort, parsley, pennyroyal, raspberry, sarsaparilla, speedwell, valerian, woodruff.

HERBAL TEAS THAT GROW IN DRY PLACES: Agrimony, blackberry, borage, burnet, chamomile, fennel, goldenrod, lavender, mullein, New Jersey tea, pennyroyal, rosemary, sage, savory (winter variety), speedwell, thyme, yarrow.

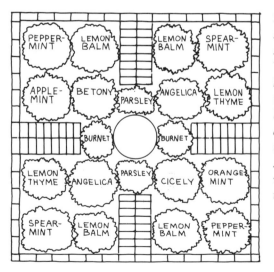

Since most herbs like full sun, planting a garden in a shady spot can be a problem. The aromatic mint family, however, provides many good teas and a fine solution. Parsley, burnet, angelica, cicely, and betony may also be added to give more color to the plot. And a statue or fountain makes a good center of interest.

A simple three-herb knot garden, adapted from traditional sixteenth-century plans. The circle can be planted in gray santolina, the square in green santolina, and the curved form in lavender. In early gardens, the spaces in between often were planted with flowers, but they also can be planted with low-growing tea herbs, such as thyme, woodruff, chamomile, dwarf marigolds, or parsley.

HERBAL TEAS FOR HEDGES: Basil, hyssop, lavender, rosemary, sage.

HERBAL TEAS FOR LOW EDGINGS: Basil (dwarf), chamomile, chrysanthemum (dwarf varieties), coltsfoot, parsley, pennyroyal, speedwell, strawberry (wild), thyme, woodruff.

HERBAL TEAS FOR GROUND COVER: *Sun:* Caraway, chamomile, coltsfoot, thyme; *shade or partial shade:* Speedwell, wintergreen, woodruff.

HERBAL TEAS FOR ROCK GARDENS OR CREVICES: Chamomile, marjoram, pennyroyal, thyme, woodruff.

TALL HERBAL TEAS: Angelica, bay, birch, elder, fennel, hawthorn, hibiscus, hollyhock, jasmine, juniper, linden, mullein, nettle, rose (large varieties), rosemary, sage, sassafras, tansy.

Herbal teas by color of the flower
(these may vary within the variety):

BLUE: Borage, flax, hyssop, speedwell.

GREEN: Nettle, sarsaparilla.

PURPLISH-BLUE: Alfalfa, lavender, lemon verbena, licorice, pennyroyal, rosemary, sage, thyme, valerian, yarrow.

PURPLISH-PINK: Oregano.

REDDISH-BROWN: Chrysanthemum varieties, mugwort.

REDDISH-PINK: Bee balm (bergamot), chrysanthemum varieties, fraxinella, hollyhock, marjoram, red clover.

REDDISH-PURPLE: Betony, burnet, mint.

VIOLET: Savory.

WHITE: Angelica, anise, balm, basil, bay, blackberry, caraway, chamomile, cicely, comfrey, elder, hawthorn, hollyhock, horehound, jasmine, Labrador tea, linden, meadowsweet, New Jersey tea, parsley, raspberry, strawberry, valerian, wintergreen, woodruff.

YELLOW: Agrimony, chrysanthemum varieties, coltsfoot, dandelion, dill, elder, fennel, fenugreek, ginseng, goldenrod, hibiscus, juniper, lemon verbena, licorice, linden, marigold, meadowsweet, mullein, tansy, yarrow.

YELLOW-GREEN: Hop, parsley, sassafras.

Once you've determined where to put your herb garden and have sketched a planting plan on paper, stake out the planting bed. Then you can prepare the soil (see chapter 2, "Guide to Cultivating Herbs").

If space permits, leave one area of the garden for reserve plants—cuttings or seedlings that are left over after you've transplanted into the garden proper. These can become replacements for herbs that don't take when you transplant or that winterkill. Also, you can gather tea ingredients from the spare herbs when you don't want to trim pampered or strategically placed plants.

If you're planning a geometric garden, mark it for planting after you've prepared the soil and edged the bed. Follow the same method you'd use if you were making geometric drawings on paper. To mark off circular areas, use a home-made compass (a stake driven into the ground, with a string and pointed marker attached to it). For straight lines, you can use a string stretched tight between two stakes, or a board, as a guideline to mark where plants should be placed.

Formal, geometrically arranged gardens gain interest if they are placed so the pattern can be seen from above (from the top of a rise, for example). Plants can also be grouped around a focal point—a sundial, birdbath, statue, or fountain. In a formal garden, the plants that delineate the design line should be small, slow-growing herbs that hold their shape. They must, of course, be trimmed and weeded regularly. Plants with less manageable foliage can be planted within the outlined spaces.

Less structured herb gardens allow for the placement of many herbs within a small area—an ideal solution for the gardener with limited space who wants plenty of variety for one-herb, two-herb, or multi-herb teas.

Protecting your herb garden in winter

If you live in an area where winters are severe, you'll want to provide protection for your perennial herbs.

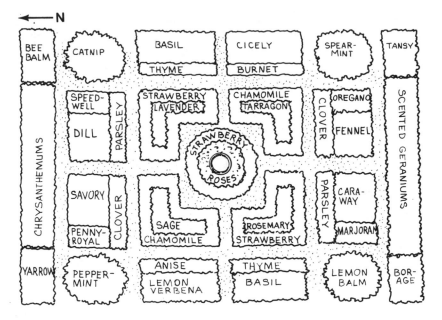

This formal herb garden provides a wide variety of herbal teas.
Taller plants at the north and south end allow sun to reach herbs
in the center beds, while gravel paths keep the plants from
spreading too much. Roses highlight a central birdbath, sundial,
or statue.

These plants are usually killed by alternate thawing and freezing, which pushes the herbs out of the ground, causing serious damage to the roots. A permanent mulch can shield delicate roots from such temperature extremes. Weed-free straw, sawdust, cocoa bean hulls, and pine bark are types of mulch you can use. The mulch should be light and porous enough to allow air to penetrate, yet thick enough to shade the soil and provide adequate insulation.

While sawdust and bark make good winter mulch, they sometimes create a nitrogen deficiency in the soil. You can correct this during the growing season by digging a little fish meal or blood meal into the soil around the plants.

One tip: Don't harvest herbal teas just before a frost. Trimming causes herbs to send out new growth, which lowers their resistance and makes them susceptible to winterkill. Try not to harvest during the month before frost is expected.

Wind can also be a problem. Even herbs that are said to be hardy in your area may be killed if winds become excessive. The wind chill factor lowers the effective temperature far below the temperature you see on your thermometer. A thermometer reading may be 0°F (− 18°C), but if there's a 30-mile-an-hour wind, the temperature your plants are experiencing is really − 49°F (− 46°C)—lower than most herbs can tolerate.

One precaution you can take is to grow plants in a protected spot on the south or west side of your house. If that's not possible, consider covering the plants completely with a mulch that won't mat them down and suffocate them. You can also create a windscreen of evergreen boughs poked into the soil around the plants, or erect a fence or pile of stones on the windward side of the garden.

Another way to ensure winter survival of perennial herbs is to grow varieties that have been developed to withstand the climate in your area. When you're buying plants, obtain them from a climate as cold as or colder than the one you'll be growing them in.

Some tender perennials (lemon verbena, bay, hibiscus, jasmine, rosemary, and the scented geraniums) must be taken into the house or moved to a warmer location (such as a porch or cold frame) when cold weather threatens. To avoid transplanting shock, grow them in pots year round, so you can bring them indoors easily in the fall. Treat these tropical varieties as house plants (see the section on indoor gardening later in this chapter). Rosemary is an evergreen; it will stay green all winter. But lemon verbena, a deciduous shrub, may drop all its leaves and become dormant during the winter. Don't throw it out because of its dead appearance—keep watering it. In the spring it will send out new leaves.

Scented geraniums need special care. Before the first killing frost, take all the cuttings you need for the following year's plants and place them in a box of clean, sharp, and slightly damp sand (perlite can be added as well). Be sure this planting container is well drained. Label each plant or row of plants, and place the cuttings vertically halfway into the sand (see the discussion of propagation by cuttings in chapter 2). Remove the planting container to the basement or to a sheltered porch, where it will remain cool and dormant until spring, but will not freeze. Then dig up the geraniums you took the cuttings from, shake off excess soil, and place them in brown paper bags. Hang these in the garage or attic. Around March, place these plants in a moist mixture of fertile green loam and peat moss. Keep them in the shade, watering them daily until color returns; then move them into sunlight. When danger of frost is past, you can plant them outdoors once again, along with the new plants that have resulted from your cuttings.

Planting the indoor garden

An indoor gardener will never be able to provide the same growing conditions that exist naturally outdoors. Apartments and houses are usually too warm, dry, and dark, and they don't supply the gentle breezes and evening dews that plants need to protect them against excessive drying and disease. Poor ventilation makes indoor plants susceptible to fungus and to attacks by aphids, mites, and other insect pests.

The challenge is to duplicate outdoor conditions as best you can. It isn't easy, but this doesn't mean you can't grow delightful herbal tea plants indoors. It just means you have to be aware of the problems and learn to overcome them.

Herbs that grow well indoors

Many herbs grow well indoors. They may not reach the fullness or height that they would outdoors (their container-bound roots are somewhat dwarfed), but they can still provide beauty and an abundance of leaves for making herbal teas.

HERBS THAT GROW WELL INDOORS: Angelica, basil, bay, borage, burnet, catnip, chamomile, dandelion, dill, fennel, horehound, jasmine, lavender, lemon balm, lemon verbena, marjoram, mint, oregano, parsley, rosemary, sage, savory, scented geraniums, tansy, tarragon, thyme, wintergreen, woodruff.

There are many choices here for the indoor herbal tea gardener who likes variety.

Choosing your window exposure

When planning your indoor garden, choose a spot where the plants will get plenty of sun—ideally a south-facing window that gets light all day. If you have a sun room, enclosed porch, or garden room, you're all set. If you don't, you may have to use artificial plant lights, giving seedlings and plants from 12 to 16 hours of artificial light each day. (See chapter 2 for more information on starting seeds and providing artificial light.)

Tender perennials should get at least as much light as they would in their native environment, whether they were brought in from the outdoors or are being cultivated inside. Consult a guide to light gardening to determine the type of equipment you should use and the amount of light you should provide in conjunction with the natural light you are working with.

You can grow a garden on a table next to a window, or in a window greenhouse. You can also grow your herbs in hanging baskets, in a terrarium, on trays, or in large window boxes. Herbs grown in pots or tubs can be used as decorative elements, too.

Watering

Give your plants enough water so the soil is moist, but not so much that they're standing in water. Root rot is caused by too much water. If you use plastic pots, you should water less. A good rule of thumb is to water regularly during warm spells, but if the air indoors is cool, wait until the surface of the soil becomes dry. The water should be at room temperature. Some herbs consume more water than others. Learn their habits, and water accordingly. The compendium of herbs later in this book will tell you which herbs like to be moist and which dry.

You should also provide enough humidity. If your home is dry, mist herbs daily, preferably early in the day. If herbs are still very damp when light is no longer available to them, they'll become susceptible to fungus (unless there is plenty of ventilation, which is hard to achieve indoors). Most herbs adapt to the drier humidity of indoor growing better than other plants.

Soil condition

Make sure indoor potting soil is porous and crumbly and provides good drainage. Commercial potting soils designed for indoor use are good; you can also make your own. Some indoor gardeners prefer a planting mix without soil—1 part peat moss and 1 part perlite or vermiculite. Then they add nutrients needed by individual plants.

Indoor plants prefer a little food given often to a lot all at once. Time-release fertilizers accomplish this, but if your pots are small and you like liquid fertilizers, choose one containing the nitrogen, phosphorus, and potassium that herbs need. Most concentrates provide dosages for once-a-month feedings. If you feed your herbs weekly, use one-quarter the amount recommended on the label. If you feed every other week, use half the amount. Fish emulsion is a favorite fertilizer of organic herb gardeners; another is seaweed extract.

Spotting poor growing conditions

If an herb's leaves wither, check to see that it's getting enough water and light. Most indoor gardeners think insects or disease are causing leaves to wither, turn brown, or develop crisp edges, but this may not be so. Perhaps the plant is getting too much heat, or soil temperatures may be fluctuating too much.

If developing leaves turn yellow, there may not be enough acidity in the soil. Remember, most herbs like a fairly neutral soil—not too acid or alkaline.

If leaves develop brown or silvery streaks, the plant may be getting too much sun. Lifeless-looking leaves may be the result of too little water. Buds dropping off usually indicates rapidly fluctuating temperatures, which is hard to remedy with indoor growing conditions. If an herb isn't blooming when it should, it's probably not getting enough sun or humidity.

If stems turn soft, the herb isn't getting enough sun, and it's probably also getting too much water.

Plant insects and diseases

Herbs growing indoors are fairly resistant to disease and insects, just as they are outdoors. But if fungus develops, treat it immediately. Otherwise the spores will spread from one plant to another via whatever insects are on the plant.

Major indoor herb pests include aphids, mealybugs, mites, and white flies. Insecticidal soaps, used to combat outside pests, are also available in indoor formulas, some with fertilizer included in their mixtures. They provide effective insect control and are organic—they contain no substances injurious to people or to pets.

Starting your garden

If you're starting plants from seed, do as you would if you were planning to put them outdoors eventually (see chapter 2), but instead transplant them to larger pots after they've developed nicely.

If you're buying nursery plants, keep them isolated from your other plants for a few days, until you've determined that they're healthy. Then you can let them get acquainted with the other herbs. Be sure to transplant herbal tea plants into larger containers as they develop.

Keep plants trimmed, not only so you can enjoy herbal teas, but also because shaping and trimming encourages them to become bushier, giving a better appearance and producing a better tea crop. Try to trim just above the leaf buds; and trim regularly rather than allowing plants to become too large and "leggy," which requires dramatic trimming. This can cause the plants to die of shock caused by the sudden imbalance between the roots and leaves.

Plan your herb pruning schedule so you can harvest an herbal tea crop when you want one.

Plants can be grouped to make an attractive garden, with a balance of textures, colors, and shapes. If the herbs are in individual containers, you can use them as decorative centerpieces for your table or as welcome fragrances in bedroom or kitchen. If the plants you use decoratively don't get sufficient light, be sure to alternate them so they are not in the shade for more than a few days at a time.

Indoor plants require careful monitoring (they depend on you for almost all their needs), but they are protected from drought, heavy downpours, and other adverse weather conditions. This means that indoor herbs are often more attractive than those grown outdoors. They offer not only beauty and fragrance close at hand, but a bountiful harvest of herbal teas as well.

4. Drying, freezing, and storing

Y OUR herbs are growing nicely. You've experimented by using fresh herbs to brew teas, but now it's time to prepare the leftovers for use when the growing season is over. How do you harvest, store, and use these herbs?

Gathering leaf teas

Gathering leaves and stems from an herb plant actually contributes to its health. If herbs are left uncut, yellow-ripe or dying leaves will result. Cutting them back promotes new growth, as well as assuring your supply of herbal delights far into the fall.

The best time for gathering leaves is on a dry, sunny morning in spring or early summer, just after the dew has evaporated—and before the sun has become hot enough to draw out the natural oils. If you pick the herbs wet, they may become moldy.

Use scissors or shears when gathering herb leaves, petals, or flowers, rather than picking them with your fingers. This helps assure clean clusters, free of adhering pieces of root. For the tenderest leaves, gather the tips of stalks rather than the full stem. If you harvest from a smaller plant, keep at least two sets of leaves at the base of each stem so the plant will continue growing. By "pruning" this way, you can obtain two or three crops of leaves in a single season.

When cutting leafy herbs—basil, savory, chervil, and marjoram—the best time of the growth cycle is just before the blossoms form, when the greatest abundance of natural oils is concentrated in the leaves. These oils will give the fullest flavor and the best leaf color when dried. After blooming, some leaf varieties change color. Savory becomes very dark, for example, and the small leaves look black and shriveled when dried. Of course, you can cut leaves after the herbs have bloomed, but the color, flavor, and texture of the leaves will be less perfect.

Using fresh herbs

If you plan to use fresh herbs, cut off dead and imperfect leaves. Wash the herbs thoroughly in clean *cold* water, then shake or towel-dry them. Remove stems wherever possible, and pop the leaves into a teapot.

Freezing leaf teas

Delicate-tasting or tender-leaved herbs—such as borage, tarragon, parsley, and basil—tend to lose some flavor in the drying process. For such plants, an excellent alternative method of preservation is freezing. Other herbs that keep especially well when frozen are marjoram, oregano, thyme, rosemary, savory, salad burnet, dill, lemon balm, lemon verbena, and mint. Before freezing, the herbs should be washed and patted dry with towels. Freeze them whole or chopped, without blanching. Plastic bags make good storage containers, because they can be stapled together and squashed into a convenient corner of the freezer. Be sure to mark each bag for later identification.

When you're ready to brew herbal tea, mince the frozen herbs on a chopping board.

Drying leaf teas

Once picked, the faster herbs are processed the better. This will ensure maximum flavor. Green herbs must be kept out of strong light and the sun to prevent the color from fading, no matter whether you plan to use them fresh, dried, or frozen. And this rule extends throughout their storage time.

You should also keep each bunch of herbs separate at all times. While you won't have any trouble telling mint from lemon balm when you're harvesting, after they are dried, one herb looks much like another. The same is true of some seeds.

If you're drying small-leaved herbs—thyme, savory, and tarragon—pick branches instead of leaves and dry them in bundles. Once they are dry it is easy to strip the leaves from the stems by running your fingers gently down either side. Other herbs that dry well in bunches are lemon balm, horehound, marjoram, and oregano. Larger leaves— mint, sage, and basil—are better if picked separately from the branches before drying. Be sure each leaf is perfect, without spots or blemishes.

Leaves gathered when the moon is waning tend to dry most rapidly, since they retain less sap in their leaves and stems. Needless to say, you should carefully avoid picking leaves that have been exposed to weed killers, car exhaust (especially if you're gathering wild herbs from the side of the road), or excessive dust.

Once gathered, the leaves should be washed quickly in cool water to remove any trace of dust and insects. Herbs that grow close to the ground—such as marjoram, parsley, and thyme—require careful handling when being washed, because they are likely to have greater deposits of soil on their leaves. Gently towel-dry the leaves after washing.

To dry herbs quickly, spread the leaves or branches on a mesh rack and place the rack in a slow oven, set at 100° to 125° F (38° to 51° C). (Higher temperatures may unfavorably influence the volatile oils in the plants.) Leave the oven door open and stand nearby, because the leaves will be chip-dry in just a few minutes. For even greater speed you may use a microwave oven, set very low, for 1 minute or less. Timing will vary with the herb and the amount being dried, so experiment with each herb and watch carefully, or you may end up with a pile of ashes. If you prefer to use a dehydrator, check the herbs frequently to determine how long they should remain in the unit.

If you do want to air-dry herbs and have the space, avoid places that could be attacked by insects or rodents. Vermin are especially troublesome in hot climates. In cold climates, mildew is a big danger.

The drying area should be dry, well ventilated, and out of direct light. In damp weather or cold climates, some artificial heat will probably be necessary to supplement the natural drying process. Outdoor sheds can be used in very dry weather, but there is always the danger of moisture seeping in at night, which will retard the drying process. Herbs that dry well hanging in bunches from a rafter or wire include sage, savory, mint, oregano, marjoram, basil, lemon balm, and horehound. Keep bunches of basil small to prevent the leaves from turning black. The flavor will remain even if they do turn, as long as they do not mold, but the tea will be unattractive. Dill may be dried this way, too, if the green leaves are desired rather than seeds.

You can also hang air-drying herbs inside brown paper bags to keep the dust off. Punch many holes into the bags to let air in and keep moisture out.

Herbs that dry well on trays, or on brown wrapping paper spread on boards, include chervil, lemon verbena, parsley, thyme, and rosemary. Parsley leaves are so thick that they can be spread only one layer deep. Thyme, however, holds so little moisture that an entire basket may be filled, and it will still dry well in any place that is not damp.

In a warm, dry spot, most herbs will air-dry in 2 days, some as quickly as overnight. Certain heavy-leafed herbs, though, may take several weeks to dry thoroughly. Even if herbs feel dry to the touch, make sure they're really free of moisture by checking them frequently after you've stored them.

Gathering and drying seeds

Seeds, the tastiest parts of many herbs, will remain vital for years, since they are naturally wrapped in sturdy covers that retain the flavorful oils. To harvest the seeds of herbs such as coriander, caraway, dill, fennel, and anise, the key word is vigilance. Seeds must be gathered when they are barely ripe—as soon as they begin to look brownish—because in a day or two the seeds will begin to drop. Then if you disturb them even slightly, they will fly in all directions, and instead of gathering this fall's harvest, you will have planted next spring's garden.

The best time of day to pick seeds is the early morning, after the dew has evaporated but while the air is relatively calm. Snip off entire seedheads with a shears, dropping them into a paper bag as you go; or cut the whole plant, if you can, and place it, seedheads down, in a paper bag. Puncture holes in the sides and top of the bag, but not the bottom. Then hang it in a warm, airy, shady place. Once the plants have dried, the seeds will usually fall to the bottom when you shake the bag.

The seeds of some plants do not ripen simultaneously; in this case you may have to pick several crops of seedheads over a week or more.

Eliminating insects

If you discover tiny insects clinging to the seeds after you've gathered them, simply drop the seedheads into boiling water for an instant. Skim off the dead insects on the surface of the water, then drain the seeds. Spread them in a single layer on tightly woven cloth towels, and put them in an airy, shady place to dry. Some seeds have tight pods or husks and do not release easily. Leave them for 2 weeks, or until you can separate the seeds from the pods or husks by rubbing them between your hands. When the seeds have been loosened, pour them through a sieve or colander to separate them from the chaff.

Gathering and drying roots

Try to gather roots when the moon is waxing, since all roots are tenderest at that time. Dig or pull up the plant, shake off excess dirt, cut off the part of the plant which was above the soil line, and wash the roots in cool water. Trim off side roots, which dry quickly and give woody fiber but little flavor. Split the roots in half lengthwise; if they're particularly large, split each piece lengthwise again. That way they'll dry more quickly.

If you are air-drying roots, process them as you would leaves. In cold climates, damp weather, or when you don't have adequate space to air-dry, you will want to oven dry. Keep the temperature 100° to 125° F (38° to 51° C) so the volatile oils won't be affected unfavorably.

To preserve flavor, keep the roots in larger pieces until you're ready to use them. At that time, grind, powder, or pound them to help release the flavors.

Gathering and drying flowers

Of course, harvesting of flowers must coincide with the flowering of the plant. Pick flowers when they are at their loveliest and most fragrant. If they're past their prime, they won't be as aromatic. Use the same directions for processing and drying flowers as for leaves.

Storing herbs

Once you've processed the leaves, flowers, roots, and seeds, you'll want to store them properly to keep them as long as possible without deterioration. Whole leaves, root pieces, and seeds retain the greatest scent and flavor. If space permits, therefore, store the herbal tea ingredients whole in airtight bottles or metal containers. If that is impossible, break them into smaller pieces, keeping in mind that the smaller the pieces, the more likely it is that aromatic oils may escape.

Herb leaves and flowers must be chip-dry when they are stored. If you processed leaves still attached to the stems, you can trim them off now, storing the leaves and discarding the stems.

Once the leaves are thoroughly dry, they must be stored immediately to preserve the essential oil that determines flavor. Seeds and roots also should be stored as soon as you determine they are thoroughly dry.

The two biggest dangers in storage are excess moisture, which produces mold, and improper sealing of storage containers, which allows vermin to contaminate your harvest. The best containers for storing herbs are jars or bottles of darkened glass fitted with glass stoppers or screw caps. If you can't find dark glass bottles, clear ones will do, but store them in a dark spot.

You may also use cans, although they are more difficult to check.

Some gardeners store herbs in paper bags, but this is the least desirable method. The herbs are not only difficult to check when stored this way, but unexpected dampness can ruin the entire harvest. Bags are also easily infested by vermin.

Be certain to keep the herbs separate, without any possibility of one mixing with another. Storage containers should be clean, and clearly labeled in indelible ink. Glue-on labels often peel off if the moisture in the air changes, so use self-adhesive labels. If you intend to preserve herbs regularly, date them as well, so you'll know which are the freshest and which may have lost their flavor. Leaf and flower herbs are best if used within 1 year, although they will keep some flavor for as long as 3 years. Seeds and roots keep longer, seeds almost indefinitely.

Jars or cans should be stored in a *cool*, dry, and dark place. Watch containers carefully for signs of condensation. If moisture appears, empty the containers at once and dry them and the herbs to prevent mold from forming.

Using dried herbs

When you're ready to use herbal leaves, break them without powdering them in order to release the maximum amount of oils. You can do this by rubbing the leaves between your hands—if they have been properly dried, they should crumble easily.

Some herbs, like rosemary, that have sharper leaves may scratch your hands if crumbled, so run them through a coffee grinder instead. They will emerge at just about the right size for use in tea. You can eliminate the residue of herbal odor by wiping the coffee grinder with the remains of a squeezed lemon or with a tissue soaked in a few drops of lemon juice.

Just before brewing root tea, break or grind the roots into small pieces, or powder them.

To prepare seeds, powder or crush them just before using. Ground seeds, like coriander and caraway, deteriorate rapidly when crushed; if they remain whole, however, they keep indefinitely. And if you have leftovers, remember almost all herb seeds will germinate if you plant them the following spring. Extra seeds also make excellent bird food during the winter.

5. How to brew herbal teas

THERE'S a knack to brewing the perfect cup of herbal tea—tea that tastes like ambrosia instead of last night's dishwater, and has the strength to refresh you without calling to mind a dose of drain cleaner.

Packaged China (*Thea sinensis*) teas, with clearly spelled-out directions, don't pose much of a problem. But because herbal teas are brewed from petals, roots, seeds, or flowers, as well as leaves—alone or in combination—they require more know-how. Once you master a few simple methods, though, it's easy to brew a cup of herbal tea with appealing aroma and satisfying taste.

The first thing you need is patience. If you don't allow ample time for brewing, you'll end up with faintly flavored hot water instead of tea. Second, you'll need to make use of your sense of taste. Unlike *Thea sinensis* teas, herbal teas do not darken as they become stronger, but remain light green or amber. The expert tea-brewer gauges the strength or weakness of herbal tea by taste rather than sight. Third, you'll need the proper brewing utensils. Basically this means a pot (preferably an enameled one with no chips) for boiling water, a teapot, a teacup, an infuser for immersing the tea in the water, a strainer, and a mortar and pestle, or grinder, to crush roots and seeds just before brewing them.

An infuser is a device that holds the tea ingredients, keeping them contained while boiling water is poured over them, so they do not flow into the teacup. Infusers are usually ball-shaped, with pin-sized holes all over their surface, and they unscrew or unhinge to open, enabling you to lock the tea ingredients inside them. Most infusers come in two sizes—one-to-two cup or six-to-eight cup. If you prefer, you can place loose ingredients into the teapot, add boiling water, and pour through a strainer to keep tea ingredients out of each cup.

The best teapots are made of china, earthenware, glass, silver, or stainless steel. Some teapots have strainers built in over the base of the spout, so you can use loose ingredients and the pot will strain the tea as you pour. Avoid tin or aluminum pots—they tend to impart a metallic taste to the tea—and never heat a teapot directly on the stove.

Depending on the type of herbal tea you're brewing, you'll use one of two methods, infusion or decoction.

Brewing by infusion

Most teas made from leaves, petals, and flowers are prepared by infusion. Infusion allows the oils in these parts of the herb to be released gently; if the herbs were boiled, the oils would evaporate.

Infusion of leaves, petals, or flowers:

1 teaspoon of dried herbs, or 3 teaspoons of freshly picked herbs to 1 cup boiling water

To infuse tea, rinse the teapot with boiling water (to heat it) and dry it thoroughly. Place tea in the pot, either loose or in its infuser, pour boiling water over the tea, and allow the mixture to steep for 3 to 5 minutes, or until the delicate flavors are released. Then strain and serve. You may add or subtract herbs according to your personal preference.

If you're using freshly picked herbs, bruise the leaves gently by crushing them in a clean cloth. This will help to release aromatic oils.

Some herbal tea experts say infused herbs should be removed and discarded as soon as the tea is made. Others believe the tea can steep for as long as a day or two.

If the herbs are allowed to sit, use boiling water to warm up the cold tea and/or dilute it if it has become too strong. A word of caution: if herbs are allowed to stand more than a day or two, they release tannic acid into the tea. Tannic acid is great for curing leather, but isn't good for delicate stomach linings. As one expert advises, "If you want your tea to be stronger, use more tea, not more time."

Brewing by decoction

The decoction method is used mainly for seed and root teas, whose oils are more difficult to release. Herbal teas prepared by decoction generally tend to stay fresher than teas prepared by other methods.

Decoction of seeds:

1 tablespoon of seeds to 1 pint (2 cups) of boiling water

Bring water to a boil in an enameled pan placed over a high heat. Add the seeds, reduce the temperature, and allow the mixture to simmer gently for 5 to 10 minutes. Then quickly strain the tea and serve it.

Seeds should be well crushed to bring out their oils. A mortar and pestle do the job nicely, or you can wrap the seeds in a clean cloth and crush them with a wooden mallet or rolling pin. You can also grind them in the type of small electric grinder used for grinding coffee beans.

Decoction of roots:

½ ounce of dried roots to 1 pint (2 cups) of boiling water

Add the powdered, ground, or crushed dried root to boiling water, reduce the temperature, and simmer for as long as it takes to brew the tea to your taste.

Ordinarily, decoction of roots takes about 20 minutes, and less if you've powdered them. A good rule of thumb is that tea will probably be ready when the water has been reduced to ½ pint (1 cup). Remove the root at this time.

Iced teas

To make iced teas, prepare them as you would hot teas, then cool them in the refrigerator.

To make a gallon (20 servings), pour 1 quart of boiling water over 2 ounces of dried herbal tea (about ¾ cup), or over 6 ounces of bruised fresh leaves. Brew 5 or 6 minutes. Stir and strain into 3 quarts of cold tap water. Serve over ice cubes.

Herbal tea concentrate for a crowd

If you want to make leaf, flower, or petal tea for a crowd, you can make a concentrate in advance, then dilute it when you're ready to serve. Here's how:

For 40 to 45 cups, bring 1½ quarts of cold water to a full rolling boil. Remove from heat. Immediately add ¼ pound of loose, dried herbal tea leaves, petals, or flowers, or ¾ pound of fresh herbs. Stir well to immerse the leaves, then cover. Let the brew steep for 5 or more minutes. Strain the concentrate into a teapot. When you are ready to serve, boil water and add it to the concentrate in cups, preparing it to taste.

Sun tea

For hundreds of years, American Indians have used the sun as a source of heat to brew herbal beverages without boiling away the natural flavor. The sun's infrared and ultraviolet rays heat the water but keep it below the boiling point. Flavor is released from the herbs, but not from the oils and acids that can give tea an acrid taste if it isn't drunk soon after brewing. This method also saves energy.

Take a large glass bottle, preferably one with a glass cover that enables the sun's rays to reach the contents easily (an old-fashioned canning jar works well). Fill the jar with water, and add tea leaves. Set the jar in the sun for 3 to 6 hours, depending on the intensity of the rays (affected by time of day) and the time of year. Remove tea residue from the water as soon as you bring the jar in from the sun. This method doesn't work for seeds and roots, which require boiling water to release their flavors.

Enhancing tea's taste

Most herbal teas are brewed to be drunk without sugar, honey, or molasses, which mask their delicate flavors. But some herbs are more tart than others, and you may want to add a sweetener. Elderberry leaves or cut fruit sweeten and add a nice flavor. So does a bit of licorice root. Dried orange peels and tangerine rinds can also be used.

Teas can also be sweetened or flavored with other teas. After you've been experimenting with herbal blends for a while (see chapter 6, "Creating Tea Blends"), you'll find you can create and brew your favorite herbal teas quickly and easily.

6. Creating tea blends

HERE comes the fun part—when you can combine two, or three, or many herbs to create teas that will delight your taste buds. Single-herb teas can be lovely, but you will be delighted with the results if you experiment by combining a few leaves of one herb and a few of another, just as people have been doing since the beginning of time.

You may not be ambitious enough to blend twenty-five or thirty herbs and spices as commercial herbal tea packagers often do. They are trying to create tastes that will appeal to the widest segment of the market, and they do an admirable job. These prepared teas, however, often contain exotic tropical herbs or spices that can't be grown in your garden.

But with what you *can* grow you can create some pretty special beverages. And they will have the distinction of being your creations, brewed from plants you've grown and processed *yourself*.

The Chippewa Indians are said to have invented the first tea bag. They would tie some herbal leaves into a little packet, using a long strip of bark to hold everything together, and then dunk it into boiling water until they had brewed palatable tea.

Today, if you'd like to mix elaborate blends and store them in bags for convenient use, you can buy empty bags that are sealed with a hot iron after you've doled out 1 teaspoon of your magic mixtures for each cup of tea.

You can also buy or make little cloth bags with drawstrings to store measured portions of your special blends. This guarantees consistency in the herbal brews, because the blends don't settle as they would in a canister.

Two-herb blends

In January 1774, a month after the Boston Tea Party, one "Philo Aletheias" wrote in the *Virginia Gazette*, "If we must through Custom have some warm Tea once or twice a day, why may we not exchange this slow poison which not only destroys our Constitutions but endangers our Liberties and drains our Country of so many thousands of Pounds a Year for Teas of our own American Plants, many of which may be found pleasant to the taste, and very salutary. . . ." He then recommended seventeen different herbal teas, including these two-herb blends:

sweet marjoram and a little mint; mother of thyme and a little hyssop; rosemary and lavender; clover with a little chamomile; sage and lemon balm leaves ("joined with a little lemon juice"); goldenrod and betony (with honey)

These were all good herbal teas for the Colonists, and are good today. (They also drank China tea taste-alikes—Labrador tea, bee balm, and New Jersey tea—which were preferred by less adventurous tea-drinkers who wanted to stick with familiar tasting beverages.)

All two-herb blends should be mixed according to personal preference, using equal parts of each herb, or more of one you like better. The blends outlined here should be brewed by infusion (1 teaspoon of dried herb, or 3 of fresh herb to 1 cup of boiling water) unless the ingredients used are entirely seeds or roots. If this is the case, brew by decoction (1 tablespoon of crushed or ground seeds or root, placed in 2 cups of boiling water and simmered until the water has been reduced to 1 cup).

Other two-herb blends which have stood the test of time include:

agrimony with licorice; alfalfa seed with mint; alfalfa leaf with lemon verbena; alfalfa leaf with red clover blossoms; angelica root with juniper berries; coltsfoot with horehound; chamomile with hibiscus flowers; dill seed with chamomile flowers; elderflowers with peppermint; elderflowers with yarrow; fenugreek with alfalfa; fenugreek with mint; hibiscus flowers with rose hips; licorice root with any other herb; marigold petals with mint; mullein with sage; mullein with marjoram; mullein with chamomile; pennyroyal with any of the other mints; peppermint with spearmint; rosemary with hibiscus flowers; strawberry leaves with woodruff; sage with lemon verbena; yarrow with peppermint

If you'd like to experiment with these blends but don't have all the ingredients, you might consider buying loose dried herbs and testing them before you decide whether to include them in your garden. Or buy those that won't grow in your area and combine them with those you can grow.

Three-herb blends

It was only a matter of time before more adventurous tea-brewers began blending three herbs. Successes included this blend, said to be an effective remedy for hangovers and nightmares:

3 parts thyme; 1 part rosemary; 1 part spearmint

Another good tea, which combines fruity and woodsy tastes, is this:

1 part strawberry leaves; 1 part blackberry leaves; 1 part woodruff

For an attractive pink tea with a lemon-spice aroma and taste, try:

1 part hibiscus petals; 1 part rose hips; 1 part lemon verbena
Add a touch of cinnamon to give a spicy accent.

Toby Chamberlain of California, a distributor of little vellum tea bags for herbal enthusiasts who grow and package their own teas, recommends this blend:

1 part dried alfalfa leaves; 1 part dried peppermint leaves; ½ part crushed caraway seeds

Multi-herb blends

Gradually your taste will begin to develop so you can judge how herbs will work together. Soon you'll know which ones enhance or complement each other, and which impart sweetness or extra tang.

Here's a good seed blend. The anise and fennel give it a licorice taste, while the coriander and caraway add an extra tang—refreshing, with a pleasant aftertaste. (I have one of those small coffee grinders that grind enough beans for a single serving. It works perfectly on herbs that need pulverizing to bring out their essential oils.)

For this one, I measure ½ teaspoon of each ingredient into the grinder, powder the seeds, and then infuse the resulting mixture:

1 part fennel seeds; 1 part anise seeds; 1 part coriander seeds; 1 part caraway seeds

Measure 1 teaspoon of the seed mixture, infuse in 2 cups of boiling water, cover, and let cool.

🌿 This one comes close to tasting like China tea, because of the bee balm and birch:

1 part ground birch leaves and twigs; 1 part peppermint; 1 part savory; 1 part bee balm (bergamot)

Infuse 1 teaspoon of the mixture in 1 cup of boiling water.

🌿 For a minty and sweet multi-herb blend combine these:

1 part catnip; 1 part chamomile; 1 part marjoram; 1 part spearmint

Infuse 1 teaspoon of dried herb mixture in 1 covered cup of boiling water for 10 minutes. Sweeten with honey if desired.

🌿 This aromatic blend has a woodsy, bittersweet scent and taste that makes a refreshing iced tea as well:

1 part sage; 1 part rosemary; 1 part hyssop; 1 part peppermint; 1 part marjoram; 2 parts thyme

Infuse in boiling water, let stand a few minutes, then enjoy.

🌿 Experimentation resulted in this tasty combination, a tangy brew similar to China tea:

1 part rose hips; 1 part hibiscus; 1 part alfalfa leaf; 1 part blackberry leaves

I grind the rose hips and hibiscus, then add the other ingredients, and infuse 1 teaspoon of blend for each cup of boiling water.

🌿 A multi-herb blend with a citrus-like taste, this tea is especially refreshing when you add a touch of dried orange peel:

1 part chamomile; 1 part rose petals; 1 part spearmint; 2 parts lemon verbena

Infuse, using 1 teaspoon of the mixture to each cup of boiling water.

🌿 A touch of orange peel and cinnamon enhance the flavors of this tea:

1 part hibiscus flowers; 1 part rose hips; 1 part lemon verbena; 1 part peppermint

Infuse to taste.

When combining fresh and dried ingredients, I use this rule of thumb for bulk: 1 part dried equals 3 parts fresh. With this tea, for example, I use 1 teaspoon dried hibiscus, and 1 teaspoon dried rose hips (both of which I grind to help release the tastes quickly). Then I add about 3 teaspoons of fresh lemon verbena from my garden, and 3 teaspoons of

fresh peppermint. Since this adds up to 4 teaspoons of dried ingredients, I infuse the mix in 4 cups of boiling water.

Here's another blend that is found in old-time herbals:

1 part meadowsweet; 1 part betony; 1 part raspberry leaves; 1 part agrimony
Infuse. Sweeten this one with honey or sugar.

To experience an old-fashioned root beer taste, try this combination:

*1 part sassafras bark; 1 part licorice root; 1 part sarsaparilla root; ½ part
wintergreen leaves*
Grind the bark and roots. Add the wintergreen, and steep for 10 minutes in
boiling water. Sweeten with honey or sugar.

My favorite creation is this apple tea, which provides a medley of
tastes:

*1 tsp. ground dried rose hips; 1 tsp. ground dried hibiscus flowers; 1 tsp. dried
chamomile flowers; 4 large fresh apple geranium leaves*
While the mixture is steeping in 4 cups of hot water, I add a pinch of
nutmeg and a pinch of cinnamon. The apple geranium gives a slightly tart
taste, so I also add honey to sweeten.

I try all kinds of herbal combinations, making one teacupful at a
time, then refining, sweetening, adding an ingredient here, or sub-
tracting one there, until the brew seems just right. I write down the
proportions of each ingredient.

You can do this, too. Soon you'll have many favorite herbal tea
recipes, with at least one for each friend or family member.

Herbal teas with spices, fruit, and liquors

Herbal teas go well with many spices, fruits, and liquors, and have
been served this way over the centuries. Here are a few old-time recipes:

Cloves and rose hips give a slightly bitter taste to this blend:

1 tsp. rose hips; 3 cloves; 3 tsp. dried lemon balm
Infuse in 2 cups of boiling water, and steep for 10 minutes. Sweeten with
honey or, for a tangier tea, add lemon juice.

Simple, sweet, and lemony, this blend is very soothing:

2 tsp. dried lemon balm; 2 cloves; 1 tsp. honey
Infuse in 2 cups of boiling water for 10 minutes.

꧁A combination which has a lavender aroma and minty taste when you're drinking it, but an aftertaste reminiscent of a China tea:

1 tsp. rosemary; 1 tsp. lavender; 1 tsp. lemon balm; 1 tsp. spearmint; 1 tsp. cloves

Mix the ingredients, and infuse 1 teaspoon of the blend for each cup of boiling water.

꧁Mace gives the usually soothing valerian tea a sharper, almost peppery taste:

1 tsp. valerian root; 1 pinch of mace

Infuse to taste in 1 cup of boiling water.

꧁A combination that's good when flavored with orange peel is this blend:

1 tsp. wood betony; 1 tsp. dandelion leaves; 1 clove

Infuse in 2 cups of boiling water.

Herbal tea ingredients spice up alcoholic drinks as well. Over the centuries many herbs have been added to wine—woodruff, for example, gives May wine its distinctive taste. By experimenting, you can create strawberry and blackberry flavored wines, as well as others. Crushed hawthorn berries are a good addition in wine or brandy.

Here's a cooling tea and liquor combination: Brew hibiscus tea until it is rich red. Then add ice until the mixture becomes light red. When thoroughly cooled, add a jigger of anisette to each glass.

An angelica liqueur can be made by chopping up and steeping 2 ounces of freshly gathered angelica stems and leaves in 2 pints of good brandy for 5 days. Then add 1 tablespoon of skinned bitter almonds ground to a pulp, stir, and strain the liquid. Add 1 pint of syrup made by boiling 2 cups of sugar in 1 cup of water for 5 minutes. Filter and bottle.

Tarragon liqueur can be made by steeping 4 teaspoonsful of fresh tarragon leaves in 1 pint of brandy for 5 days. Then make a syrup of ¾ cup of sugar boiled in just enough water to dissolve it, and add to the blend. Before bottling this mixture, add 1 ounce of orange flower water.

Purists may argue some of these combinations aren't truly teas, because the herbal ingredients are not infused in hot water. However, dictionary definitions of *infusion* and *tea* often mention herbs being steeped "in liquids." While the semanticists argue, you can try them out. These recipes are slightly more ambitious, and their success depends on long periods of steeping.

✎ Dandelion tea becomes a tasty wine with this recipe:

16 cups of dandelion flowerheads; 1 gallon water; 2 oranges; 1 lemon; 1 oz. ginger root; 4 pounds sugar; ½ oz. yeast; 1 egg white (optional)

Use only fresh dandelion blossoms from which you have removed all stems—otherwise the wine will be bitter. Slice the oranges and lemon. Place dandelion heads, water, oranges, lemon, and ginger (crushed and tied in a muslin bag) in a pan, and bring the mixture to a boil. Boil for 20 minutes. Strain and add the sugar. If the mixture isn't clear, add the white of an egg. Place the yeast into the mixture, and let set for a week. Then strain and bottle, capping the bottles loosely for a few days, then more tightly. Let this blend stand for 6 months before using.

✎ If you start elderflower wine today, you can enjoy it 6 months from now:

4 cups fresh elderflower blossoms; 3 gals. water; 9 lbs. sugar; 2 tsp. lemon juice; 1 yeast cake; 3 lbs. raisins

Boil the water and sugar together, then pour over the blossoms. Allow to cool, then add lemon juice and yeast. Put the mixture into a crock, and let it stand 9 days. Strain through cheesecloth, and add the raisins. Put the mix back into the crock, and allow it to stand for 6 months. Then strain and bottle.

Herbs with China tea

You can experiment with all herbs in combination with the China teas. Here are a few favorites:

1 bag of China tea; 3 cloves; 2 rose geranium leaves

Steep in 1 cup of boiling water.

✎ Honey and mint give a sweet, cool taste to this combination:

1 tsp. green tea; 3 tsp. fresh mint (or 1 tsp. dried mint); 1 tsp. honey

Infuse in 2 cups of boiling water.

✎ Raspberry leaves give a tart, fruity taste to this combination, so you may want to sweeten it with honey or sugar:

1 tsp. China tea; 1 tsp. dried raspberry leaves

Infuse in 2 cups of boiling water.

❧Bee balm makes this blend aromatic and tasty:

1 part China tea; 1 part bee balm (bergamot)
Infuse 1 teaspoon of mixture to each cup of boiling water.

❧A warm, sweet, and slightly lemony taste characterizes this tea:

1 part China tea; 1 part hibiscus flowers
Infuse. This blend is particularly good when iced.

Coffee substitute

For those who want the taste of coffee but no caffeine, here's an old-time substitute, used when imported coffee beans were not available:

1 tsp. ground roasted dandelion root; ½ tsp. chicory
Infuse in 1 cup of boiling water. This combination tastes a lot like coffee and is good either black or with cream and sugar.

Herbal punches

Here are two favorite punches made from herbal teas:

❧Lemon Balm Punch:

Pour 2 quarts of boiling water over 2 big handfuls of fresh lemon balm leaves. Allow to steep for 20 minutes, then strain. Add 2 tablespoons of honey and allow the mixture to cool. Just before serving, add ice and 1 quart of ginger ale. Float sprays of mint on top. Serves about 15.

❧Mintale (a popular punch with the French):

1 cup equal parts orange mint, apple mint, and spearmint; 2 cups boiling water; 2 tbsp. sugar; 1 large bottle of ginger ale; juice of 1 orange and 1 lemon
Infuse the mint in the 2 cups of boiling water. Cool and add the other ingredients plus ice. Float sprigs of apple mint on top of the punch.

As you can see, you can make endless numbers of creative and tasty beverages with herbal teas. Try these and concoct your own!

7. Compendium of herbs

THIS compendium of herbs is designed to provide the information you'll need to grow and brew each of seventy herbal tea plants. The chart at the end of this chapter gives capsulized data on these herbs for quick reference or comparison.

In gathering this data, I drew on my own experience and on the research of horticulturists, historians, and medical specialists over the centuries. Often there were sharp differences of opinion among the experts about such details as soil, sunlight, and applications. In the end, I let the preponderance of opinion and my own good sense be my guide. That's what you'll have to do, too. The herbs you wish to grow may prefer an environment you can't provide, but they may be maverick enough to thrive in what you offer them.

At least one grower insists that you must talk to herbs regularly if you want them to respond. Another believes that herbs must be planted with serious regard for their astrological signs. What seems right to you is probably best. If it works, fine. If it doesn't, try something else.

When it comes to *brewing* individual teas, there are also differences of opinion. Tastes vary, and you should experiment until you find what suits you.

Some of the herbs in the book are controversial. They were on the FDA's "hit list," published a few years ago, of herbs said to be harmful to humans. But, some of the disputed herbs (sassafras, catnip, and valerian, for example) continue to be very popular. To omit them from the compendium would be like eliminating lipstick from a book on cosmetics. (Remember a few years ago, the FDA announced that lipstick may cause cancer!) So the controversial herbs are included here with appropriate cautions. As with any food or beverage, it is not only wise, but also more exciting, to try many teas in moderation rather than one or two in excess. If you do, you will embark on an odyssey of discovery through the wide world of herbal teas.

Agrimony *(Agrimonia eupatoria)*

Agrimony's common names in Britain are Sticklewort, Cockleburr, and Church Steeples (because of the herb's yellow spire-like flowers). Pronounced with emphasis on the first syllable, its generic name comes from the Greek word *argemone* (meaning "a plant that heals the eyes"), and *eupatoria* from Mithridates Eupator, king of Pontus, who practiced immunotherapy. Agrimony and related species can be found wild throughout Europe, in Canada, and in the United States, where its natural habitats are woods, fields, and hedgerows. The tea was once used as a substitute for *Thea sinensis*, and it is a favorite beverage in France. Agrimony tea is believed to alleviate gout, and it makes a good gargle for mouth and throat inflammations. It is said to relieve chronic gall-bladder problems and constipation and to strengthen the liver. During the Middle Ages, agrimony was thought to have magic powers and was placed under the pillow to induce deep sleep.

PLANT: A hardy perennial. Its reddish, creeping roots produce a stem covered with fine silky down and widely spaced opposite leaves similar to those of a wild rose. Small yellow flowers bloom at the top of the stem from June to September, and the fruiting flower tubes have hooked bristles.

HEIGHT: To 5 feet, usually about 3 feet.

SOIL: Well-drained, ordinary soil on the dry side.

EXPOSURE: Full sun or light shade.

PROPAGATION: Seeds planted in spring or fall during the third lunar phase. Also by root division. Agrimony's seed pod, a bristly burr, is distributed when it catches the fur of animals or clothes of passersby. It germinates easily and, once established, sows itself.

CARE: Space mature plants 7 to 10 inches apart.

PART USED FOR TEA: Flowers, leaves, and stems harvested when the plant is in flower. When crushed, the flowers and leaves give off a faint lemony scent.

TASTE: Reminiscent of apricots. Good when flavored with licorice or honey.

How to brew

BY INFUSION: Steep 1 to 2 teaspoons of dried herb in 1 cup of boiling water, or 3 teaspoons of fresh herb, gently crushed.

Alfalfa *(Medicago sativa)*

Alfalfa is also known as Lucerne, Buffalo Herb, and, because of its bluish or purple flowers, Purple Medick. A leguminous plant, with roots that go deep into the soil, it is a rich source of fourteen of the sixteen principal mineral elements, particularly iron, phosphorus, potassium, and magnesium. Alfalfa also contains vitamins A, D, E, G, and K. The herb is said to give race horses speed and athletes stamina. It is also believed to relieve arthritis and other twinges and pains, to stimulate appetite, to build the body, and to help in the treatment of alcohol and drug addiction. Alfalfa is thought to aid digestion and elimination and to help cure peptic ulcers.

PLANT: A hardy perennial, the clover-like plant has an erect smooth stem, which grows from an elongated taproot. Oblong leaflets grow in groups of three around the stem. The plant is found on the borders of fields and in low valleys, and it is widely cultivated for fodder and as a soil builder (it increases the nitrogen content of the soil with the help of nitrogen-fixing bacteria, which enter the root hairs and form nodules that nurture the plant and surrounding soil). Purplish flowers grow in racemes—many small flowers growing off the stem —and bloom from June to August. Spirally coiled seed pods follow.

HEIGHT: 1 to 3 feet.

SOIL: Well-drained soil of reasonably good fertility, slightly acid.

Exposure: Full or partial sun.

Propagation: Seeds sown in early spring or late summer during the third lunar phase.

Care: Space plants 8 to 10 inches apart. Make sure there is no hardpan or underlying rock layer where you plant it, because alfalfa sends its roots down deep. Researchers have traced them for well over 100 feet—20 to 30 feet is average.

Part used for tea: Leaves and seeds.

Taste: Bland, tastes like newly mown hay. It is usually blended with mint, lemon verbena, red clover, or honey.

How to brew

Leaves, by infusion: 1 teaspoon of dried herb or 3 teaspoons of fresh crushed herb, to 1 cup of boiling water. Steep to taste.

Seeds, by decoction: Crush 1 tablespoon of seeds, and add to 2 cups of boiling water. Reduce temperature and allow mixture to simmer gently for 5 to 10 minutes.

Angelica *(Angelica archangelica)*

Angelica is also commonly known as Masterwort, Archangel, Holy Ghost Plant, and St. Michael's Plant, since it blooms on his day (May 8) in many parts of the world. Believed to be native to Syria, angelica is said to be a remedy for colds, coughs, pleurisy, flatulence, rheumatism, and fevers. In the fifteenth and sixteenth centuries, herbalists thought a bag of angelica leaves tied around a child's neck would protect against witchcraft and evil spells.

PLANT: Angelica is considered a biennial, but it will continue to live several years if the flower stems are clipped off before they bloom. The stem is round, hollow, and grooved, branching near the top, where it is tinged with blue. The brown to red-brown roots have a spicy, agreeable odor and taste that is sweet at first, then bitter and sharp. The seeds and an oil made from the stems and roots are used as a flavoring in many liqueurs. Leaves grow from dilated sheaths that surround the stem. Greenish-white honey-smelling flowers grow in umbrella-shaped bunches, flowering from June to August. The fruit is oblong, and breaks apart when ripe into a pair of yellow winged seed-cases, commonly called seeds.

HEIGHT: 4 to 6 feet.

SOIL: Moist, rich soil, slightly acid.

EXPOSURE: Preferably partial shade.

PROPAGATION: Seeds planted in fall during the third or fourth lunar phase. Seeds must be sown within a few weeks

after ripening; otherwise, they lose their ability to germinate. They self-sow as well. Angelica can also be propagated from root cuttings.

CARE: Space about 3 feet apart. It is best to harvest leaves before the plant flowers, while they are still tender.

PART USED FOR TEA: Leaves, seeds, sometimes roots.

TASTE: Resembles China tea in flavor, with a slight celery taste. If seeds or roots are used, they're often boiled along with juniper berries. Leaf tea is good with honey or lemon.

How to brew

LEAVES, BY INFUSION: 1 teaspoon of dried herb, or 3 teaspoons of fresh crushed herb, to 1 cup of boiling water. Steep to taste.

SEEDS OR ROOTS, BY DECOCTION: Crush or grind 1 tablespoon of seeds, or 1 ounce of root, and add to 2 cups of boiling water. Reduce temperature and allow the mixture to simmer gently for 5 to 10 minutes or longer to taste.

Anise (*Pimpinella anisum*)

Pronounced with emphasis on the first syllable, anise is sometimes called Aniseed, and was widely used in the sixteenth century as mousetrap bait, since mice could not resist it. Many humans find it irresistible, too. Originally from Greece and Egypt, anise traveled with the Romans to Europe and England and was one of the first herbs to be brought to America. It is widely cultivated. Anise tea is considered helpful in the treatment of asthma, colic, bronchitis, and nausea. It is also believed to promote milk production in nursing mothers, to induce sleep, and to bring on menstruation. It is widely used as a flavoring agent in candies and liqueurs.

PLANT: Annual. Anise has two types of leaves: those that grow thickly at the base of the stem and are bright green, oval, and tooth-edged, and those on the stems, which are smaller, elongated leaves, each divided into three segments. Tiny white flowers grow in thick, umbrella-like clusters at the tops of the stems. Seeds are light-colored and crescent-shaped, and a small piece of stem clings to them after harvesting.

HEIGHT: 2 feet.

SOIL: Light, fairly well-worked soil, enriched with compost.

EXPOSURE: Full sun.

PROPAGATION: By seed, sown in spring during the first or second lunar phase after the days and nights are frost-free.

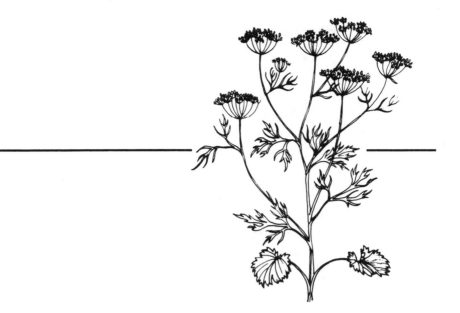

Anise needs 70°F (21°C) temperature to germinate and 120 days of frost-free weather to mature. It should be sown where it is to grow because the plant has a taproot and doesn't transplant well after it is established.

CARE: A slow-growing plant, which tends to lie down, anise requires continual weeding. Plants should be spaced 8 inches apart. Thin out seedlings or pinch off at the ground.

PART USED FOR TEA: Leaves and seeds.

TASTE: Aromatic and sweet with a licorice-like taste. Good brewed with warm milk and drunk just before going to bed.

How to brew

LEAVES, BY INFUSION: 1 teaspoon of dried leaf, or 3 teaspoons of fresh, crushed leaf, to 1 cup of boiling water. Allow to steep.

SEEDS, BY DECOCTION: Crush or grind 1 tablespoon of the seeds, and add to 2 cups of boiling water. Reduce temperature and allow mixture to simmer gently for 5 to 10 minutes.

Balm *(Melissa officinalis)*

Other names for this herb are Lemon Balm, Balm Mint, Blue Balm, Cure-All, Dropsy Plant, Honey Plant, Melissa, and Sweet Balm. Balm is a symbol of sympathy and gentleness. Linnaeus named it *Melissa,* the Greek word for "bee," because of bees' attraction to it. Common in the Mediterranean area and the Near East, it is also naturalized in some parts of the United States, where it grows wild in fields and gardens and along roadsides. The ancients believed balm tea would ensure long life. It is also thought to relieve colic, cramps, bronchial catarrh, dyspepsia, and some forms of asthma. As a warm infusion, it is used for migraine and toothache, and for the headaches and dizziness of pregnancy. And balm tea is also said to dispel melancholy and sadness.

PLANT: Perennial, hardy to − 20°F (− 29°C). The light green leaves are heavily veined, 2 to 3 inches long, with scalloped edges. The leaves are intensely fragrant, with a lemony smell. Small white flowers grow along the stems, but they are not numerous.

HEIGHT: 1½ to 4 feet.

SOIL: Medium-dry, poor, light sandy soil if you don't want lots of spreading; moist, richer soil if you want to encourage wide spreading.

EXPOSURE: Sun or partial shade.

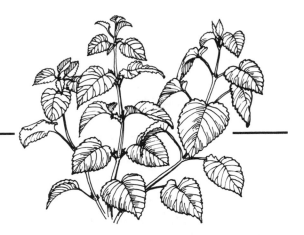

PROPAGATION: By root division or cuttings in spring or fall. Also by seeds planted during the third lunar phase. Seeds are viable for 3 or 4 years, but they take 14 to 21 days to germinate.

CARE: Space mature plants 18 inches apart. Pinch tops back to increase foliage and to keep flowers from going to seed. Keep weeded. If plants spread out too much, shear them back to contain them. Small plants can be transplanted.

PART USED FOR TEA: Leaves.

TASTE: Lemony, refreshing.

How to brew

BY INFUSION: Pick leaves that have not set flower buds. Do this early in the day, while the leaves are still rich with aromatic oils. Use 2 teaspoons of dried leaves or 4 teaspoons of crushed fresh leaves. Place in a warmed porcelain pot, pour in 1 cup of boiling water, and steep to taste. Can be flavored with sugar, honey, and/or a twist of lemon.

Basil (*Ocimum basilicum*)

Basil, also known as Common Basil, St. Josephwort, and Sweet Basil, is found wild in tropical and subtropical regions of the world. It is the focus of a centuries-old controversy: some attribute evil powers to it, and others hold it as an object of sacred worship. Its name, which rhymes with "dazzle," derives from *basileus*, the Greek word for "king," and it is highly esteemed in the East, where it is planted outside Hindu temples. In Crete, however, basil is considered an ill omen and an agent of the Devil. The herb's usefulness is generally associated with the stomach and related organs. Basil is believed to relieve stomach cramps, enteritis, constipation, vomiting, and gastrointestinal catarrh. It is also believed to promote lactation in nursing mothers.

PLANT: Annual. Basil's shiny green leaves are 1 to 2 inches long, and small white flowers grow in spikes at the ends of the stems.

HEIGHT: 1 to 2 feet.

SOIL: Moderately rich, moist, well-composted.

EXPOSURE: Full sun or semi-shade.

PROPAGATION: From stem cuttings, or from seeds sown in late spring, during the first or second lunar phase, at a minimum temperature of 60°F (15°C). Germination is quick at higher temperatures. Seedlings may "damp off" if planted too thickly, so sow seeds thinly. A light covering of clean

sand sprinkled over the soil will absorb excess moisture. If you're starting seeds indoors, use a fungicidal powder dissolved in the water you use to saturate the planting mixture.

CARE: Don't transplant seedlings started indoors to the garden until the days *and* nights are warm. Mature plants should be 12 inches apart, and they should be pinched back frequently to promote bushiness. Also, pinch off flower buds to keep the plant from becoming tough. Basil should not be fertilized, as its flavor is likely to be affected. It's a popular choice for planting near patios because its scent repels flies and mosquitoes.

PART USED FOR TEA: Leaves.

TASTE: Spicy, clove-like flavor.

How to brew

BY INFUSION: Use 1 teaspoon of dried herb or 3 teaspoons of fresh, crushed herb. Cover with 1 cup of boiling water and flavor with honey if desired.

Bay *(Laurus nobilis)*

Bay is known by many other common names: Laurel, Grecian Laurel, Indian Bay, Sweet Bay. It is an evergreen bush or tree, found both wild and cultivated around the Mediterranean Sea. In ancient Greece, laurel leaves were used to make crowns for Olympic heroes and poets, and the tree was considered sacred to the god Apollo. Bay grows widely in the Pacific Northwest and in other warm-temperature and subtropical climates. It is not winter hardy, and it must be grown as a pot plant in colder climates and taken indoors during the cold seasons. Bay tea is used as an astringent, and it is said to aid digestion, relieve flatulence, and stimulate appetite. It is also believed to protect the user from witchcraft and to ease the pains of childbirth.

PLANT: Tender, perennial tree with smooth-barked trunk, and thick, shiny, dark evergreen leaves. Whitish flowers are small, grow in clusters, and are seldom seen in the North. Flowers appear in April and May and develop into black, egg-shaped berries.

HEIGHT: 3 to 6 feet when cultivated as a pot shrub. Up to 30 feet when grown outdoors in temperate climate.

SOIL: Sandy, well-drained.

EXPOSURE: Full sun or partial shade. Protect from cold winds.

PROPAGATION: By stem cuttings. Take 3- to 4-inch-long shoots of half-ripened stems, and place them in soil of sand and peat moss in a shady place outdoors. Or, shoots may be

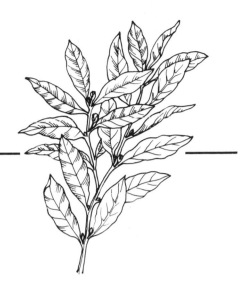

layered. Allow 6 months or more for rooting. Suckers — shoots rising from a subterranean stem or root—develop a good root system more quickly.

CARE: If using as a bush outdoors, place plants 4 feet apart, and prune to desired height. As a pot plant, prune to promote bushiness, and bring indoors during colder weather. Bay grows very slowly, so bay trees are seldom inexpensive.

PART USED FOR TEA: Leaves.

TASTE: Pungent, almost bitter. Can be sweetened with honey.

CAUTION: Only *Laurus nobilis* and *Magnolia glauca* varieties are used as foodstuffs, and both are said to have narcotic properties, so they should be used sparingly. Native laurels are poisonous and should not be used at all.

How to brew

BY INFUSION: Use 1 teaspoon of dried leaves or 3 teaspoons of fresh crushed leaves. Cover with 1 cup of boiling water, and steep to taste.

Bee Balm (Monarda didyma)

Bee Balm is known by other names: Bergamot, Oswego Tea, Monarda, Blue Balm, Scarlet Monarda, High Balm, Low Balm, Mountain Balm, and Mountain Mint. The genus name Monarda honors the sixteenth-century Spanish botanist and physician Nicolas Monardes, who wrote about medicinal and useful herbs. Bee balm is a true American wildflower and a member of the mint family. Its native habitats are moist areas and stream banks, and it is found from Georgia and Tennessee northward and as far west as Michigan and Ontario. The red-flowered monarda was known to the American Indians and early settlers, who made a hot beverage of the leaves and flowers. It became a special favorite after the Boston Tea Party, since it was the closest taste substitute for China tea. Bee balm is said to relieve nausea, vomiting, and flatulence. Because it is rich in a substance called thymol, which has a pungent taste and odor, the herb is used extensively in modern medicine and dentistry as an aromatic antiseptic.

PLANT: Perennial. Its hard, square, grooved stems have 3- to 6-inch rough, dark, paired leaves branching off from them. The delightful, scarlet, two-lipped flowers are beloved by long-tongued bumblebees and butterflies but are the despair of honeybees, who cannot reach the nectar deep in the flowers. Flowers bloom in solitary terminal heads, July to September.

HEIGHT: 1 to 3 feet.

SOIL: Moist, swamp-type soil; moderately acid.

EXPOSURE: Full sun or partial shade.

PROPAGATION: By seeds, stem cuttings, or root division. Seeds should be planted during the third lunar phase; root divisions should be made in the spring. If the plants are divided later, they're apt to winterkill.

CARE: Mature plants should be spaced 18 inches apart. Plants spread quickly so they should be taken up every 3 years, divided, and reset. Replant only the outside, newer roots; discard exhausted central plants. To increase flower size, do not let plants flower the first summer. In successive years, cut back the plant after it blooms, and it will flower again in early autumn. Late in autumn, cut down the stalks, and cover the roots with enriched soil.

PART USED FOR TEA: Leaves, flowers. Be sure to wash flowers well in order to float out insects lurking in the deep corollas.

TASTE: Aromatic, minty.

How to brew

BY INFUSION: Steep 1 teaspoon dried leaves or flowers in 1 cup of boiling water for 15 minutes. Strain. Add honey to flavor.

Betony *(Stachys officinalis)*

Pronounced with emphasis on the first syllable, betony also goes by many other common names: Lousewort, Bishopwort, Purple Betony, and Wood Betony. The botanical word for this herb comes from the Greek word *stachys*, meaning "spike," because of the arrangement of its blooms. Betony is native to open woodlands and heaths from Scotland to the Mediterranean and from Spain to the Caucasus. Sir William Hookers (the first director of the Royal Botanical Gardens, Kew, Surrey) claimed the English name *betony* is a corruption of the Celtic words *bew* ("head") and *ton* ("tonic"); the herb's tea is believed to relieve nervous headaches and tension. Older herbals claim betony purifies the blood and is a fine, natural painkiller. In European monasteries, it was used to treat shortness of breath. The Saxons believed chewing betony leaves before a party would prevent drunkenness, and an infusion was supposed to prevent bad dreams.

PLANT: Hardy perennial. The hairy, unbranched, or slightly branched stems have opposite leaves that are oblong at the bottom of the plant and lance-shaped closer to the top. Whorls of red-purple flowers bloom from July to August. The plant has a musky odor.

HEIGHT: 8 to 24 inches.

SOIL: Deep, fertile, well-drained. Moderately moist.

EXPOSURE: Full sun or partial shade.

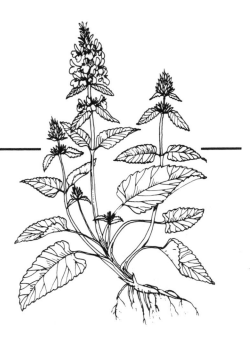

PROPAGATION: Seeds or "nutlets" that fall free around the plant are sown in fall, or in spring during the third lunar phase. Also by root cuttings.

CARE: Betony is a slow grower. The plants may benefit from division and replanting every third or fourth year. However, if they're thriving and blooming well, leave them alone.

PART USED FOR TEA: Leaves.

TASTE: Pleasant, warm, astringent. Slightly bitter, so you may want to sweeten with honey.

How to brew

BY INFUSION: 1 teaspoon of dried leaf or 3 teaspoons of crushed fresh leaf. Place in a porcelain pot, cover with 1 cup of boiling water, then steep to taste. Don't overindulge — betony tea made from fresh leaves can have a rather intoxicating effect!

Birch *(Betula alba)*

This herb is also called Cherry Birch, Sweet Birch, or White Birch. The word *birch* is said to come from the Sanskrit *bhurga* meaning "tree whose bark is written on." Birches have long been a symbol of the return of spring, and several species are found throughout cooler parts of the Northern Hemisphere. Coleridge called the birch "Lady of the Woods." The oil in birch tea is believed to purify the blood, relieve rheumatism, and expel worms. A standard infusion is used to treat skin complaints, including stubborn cases of acne, itching, and eczema.

PLANT: A deciduous tree. Young birches have dark bark; they do not develop the characteristic white bark until they are several years old. The tree has drooping branches, and the white bark peels off easily. The branches produce catkins containing either male or female flowers.

HEIGHT: To 60 feet. It is a slow grower.

SOIL: Dry or moist sandy soil.

EXPOSURE: Full sun.

PROPAGATION: From seeds sown in sandy soil during the third lunar phase or by green stem cuttings.

CARE: If you buy a tree at a nursery, be sure to water it thoroughly at least once a week. Don't let the soil become dry because water allows the roots to take up moisture and send out new growth. Birches improve soil, restoring fertility

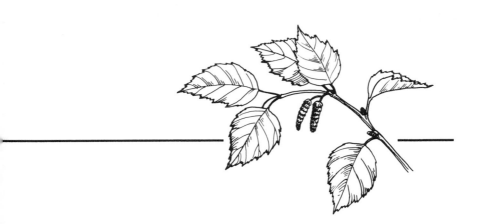

to barren areas. However, in the forest, they are fertilized by rich organic material that is constantly replenished by humus from decaying leaves. To make up for this lack of soil fertility in a garden situation, and to ensure moisture, the tree should be mulched with leaf compost. Every 2 or 3 years, it should be fertilized with a solution of nitrates, phosphates, and potash.

PART USED FOR TEA: Leaves, twigs, or bark.

TASTE: Like wintergreen in flavor, very aromatic. Birch tea can be sweetened with honey.

How to brew

BY INFUSION: If using leaves, 1 teaspoon of dried leaves, or 3 teaspoons of crushed fresh leaves, to 1 cup of boiling water. Steep to taste. If you're using twigs or bark, measure 3 teaspoons of fresh or dried herb, crush it, and allow more time for steeping, so oils can be released from the tougher fiber.

Blackberry *(Rubus* species)

Common names for this herb also include Brambleberry, Cloudberry, Dewberry, Goutberry, and Thimbleberry. One botanist termed the blackberry "the plant of Venus in Aries," and said, "If any ask the reason why Venus is so prickley, tell them 'tis because she is in the house of Mars." Blackberry bushes are found worldwide and are often cultivated. *Rubus villosus*, the type of plant most commonly used for tea, is a shrubby vine found wild in hedgerows, woodlands, and by streams. The tannic qualities of the leaves have made it a long-standing home remedy for diarrhea. The tea is believed to relieve inflammation of the intestines and catarrhal disorders, and it is popularly used as an astringent or tonic. Others feel it helps to purify offensive saliva, cool the blood, and cure anemia and general debility.

PLANT: A tender perennial. It is distinguished by its slender, trailing, prickly branches and leaves covered with fine hairs. The 1-inch broad, white, rose-form flowers appear from May to July, followed by big, juicy, black fruits — favorites for eating and for making wine and brandy.

HEIGHT: The shrub (not counting the long trailers) grows from 3 to 6 feet.

SOIL: Dry, sandy.

EXPOSURE: Direct sun, or partial shade.

PROPAGATION: By seeds planted during the third lunar phase, stem cuttings, or root cuttings. It can also be propagated by layering.

CARE: Space plants 3 to 5 feet apart along rows that are 6 feet apart. In northern areas protect with leaves or soil in cold weather. Keep well pruned for good berry yield and a more compact plant. *Rubus* flowers appear on the wood of second-year growth. (First-year stems are sterile.) Remove old canes after the fruit has been harvested.

PART USED FOR TEA: Leaves.

TASTE: Tangy and pleasant with a cool, refreshing aftertaste. Commonly sweetened with honey. A favorite combination is equal parts of the leaves of blackberry, strawberry, and woodruff.

How to brew

BY INFUSION: Cover 1 teaspoon of dried leaves, or 3 teaspoons of fresh leaves, with 1 cup of boiling water. Steep to taste.

Borage *(Borago officinalis)*

Pronounced to rhyme with "porridge," borage is also commonly called Burrage and Common Bugloss. Borage grows wild in the Mediterranean countries. It once had a reputation for dispelling melancholy and giving courage, so the ancient Greeks put it into their wine. It is also believed to have some calming effects, useful for treatment of nervous conditions, and the leaves are said to stimulate lactation in nursing mothers. Borage is thought good for reducing fever and restoring vitality during recovery from illness. Because it enhances perspiration, it is also credited with some antidotal effect against poisons. Astrologers place borage under Jupiter's realm and under the zodiac sign of Leo, the lion.

PLANT: Annual. Borage is a spreading, branched plant covered with sharp, whitish bristles. The large leaves (up to 12 inches long) are oval or oblong, and blue flowers with dark anthers nod downward in leafy clusters at the tips of the stems. Borage is ideal planted in borders and in containers where its lovely flowers can be seen close up.

HEIGHT: 1 to 3 feet.

SOIL: Dry, somewhat poor.

EXPOSURE: Sun or filtered shade.

PROPAGATION: By seeds planted in spring during the first or second lunar phase. They germinate quickly. Borage self-seeds easily, and it can become a pest in mild climates.

CARE: The plants take up a lot of room. Because they have a taproot, they don't transplant well. They should be placed at least 1 foot apart or thinned. Planting them near tomatoes is said to control tomato worms.

PART USED FOR TEA: Leaves, flowers.

TASTE: Pleasant, cucumber-like. Some say it is cooling, others that it's spicy hot. Try it yourself to judge.

How to brew

BY INFUSION: 1 teaspoon of dried leaves and/or flowers or, preferably, 3 teaspoons of fresh herb gathered in the morning just after the dew is off the plants, when the oils are strongest. Crush the fresh herb with a clean cloth to help release aromatic oils. Add 1 cup of boiling water, and steep to taste.

Burnet *(Sanguisorba minor or Poterium sanguisorba)*

Burnet is pronounced with emphasis on the first syllable.
There's some confusion about this herb, with many botanists
referring to two cousins, Salad Burnet and Garden Burnet,
by the same names. Both varieties have been valued for their
healing qualities. Growing in sheltered valleys in Europe,
North America, and Asia, burnet is supposed to slow the
flow of internal and external bleeding, and legend says King
Csaba of Hungary used it to help heal the wounds of 15,000
soldiers after a great battle. Burnet tea is also reputed to have
been drunk by American soldiers during the Revolutionary
War on nights before they were to enter battle to help keep
them from bleeding to death if they were wounded. The herb
is also believed to be an aid in relieving dysentery. At one
time, it was used to flavor wine.

PLANT: Perennial, hardy to − 30°F (− 34°C). Burnet has small,
nearly evergreen, compound leaves that consist of several
pairs of sharply serrated leaflets set in opposite pairs along
the leaf stalks. The flowers are clustered at the ends of stems
rising above the leaves. They are tiny, thimble-shaped, and
deep red or purple in color.

HEIGHT: 1 to 2 feet.

SOIL: Average, well-drained, sandy or chalky.

EXPOSURE: Full sun.

PROPAGATION: By seeds planted ½ inch deep during the
third lunar phase in fall, as soon as they are ripe, or during

the third lunar phase in early spring. Germination is slow. The plant self-sows freely, and seedlings can be moved when small. Once established, burnet can also be propagated by root division.

CARE: Place plants 12 inches apart. They make an attractive ground cover, and continue to supply greens if the flower stems and leaves are continually cut back. Burnet begins growing in March and can be harvested until after the first snowfall. Its ability to remain green throughout the winter, even when growing in poor soil, at one time made burnet a popular fodder plant in Great Britain.

PART USED FOR TEA: Leaves.

TASTE: Cucumber-like (similar to borage) if fresh, new leaves are used; less cucumber-like and nuttier if leaves have been dried.

How to brew

BY INFUSION: 1 teaspoon of dried leaves, or 1 tablespoon of fresh crushed leaves, steeped in 1 cup of boiling water.

Caraway *(Carum carvi)*

Often called by its German name, Kümmel or Kuemmel, this plant's crescent-shaped seeds are reputed to strengthen the memory and to prevent lovers from being fickle. The ancient Greeks prescribed caraway tea for pale young girls, in the belief it would bring color to their cheeks. Caraway seeds flavor kummel liqueurs, which many people make themselves by steeping 2 tablespoons of crushed caraway seeds and 1 cup of powdered sugar in 1 pint of brandy. This mixture is shaken daily for a week, after which it is strained and used. Caraway tea is believed to stimulate appetite and digestion, to promote the onset of menstruation, to relieve uterine cramps, and to increase lactation. It has also been used for flatulent colic in infants and as a stomach settler for those who have taken nauseous medicines.

PLANT: Biennial, hardy to − 30°F (− 34°C). It has delicate, lacy foliage, similar to that of the carrot, which grows on a hollow stem. The white carrot-shaped root is sometimes eaten as a vegetable. Flat, umbrella-like clusters of greenish-white flowers appear in May and June on stems that rise above the foliage. The seeds (fruit) are dark brown, oblong, and flattened, and they must be gathered after they have ripened but before they fall to the ground.

HEIGHT: 2 feet.

SOIL: Neutral, well-drained.

EXPOSURE: Full sun.

94

PROPAGATION: By seeds, planted ¼ inch deep during the third or fourth lunar phase in fall or spring. Germination is slow. Fall planting will yield plants the following year. Spring planting will delay seed formation until the second year.

CARE: Keep plants 8 inches apart. The seeds ripen unevenly, and care must be taken to harvest them regularly. In cold climates, protect the plants with mulch in winter.

PART USED FOR TEA: Seeds.

TASTE: Warm, sweet, biting.

How to brew

SEEDS, BY INFUSION: Grind or crush 1 teaspoon of seed. Cover with 1 cup of boiling water. Steep to taste.

SEEDS, BY DECOCTION: Use 2 teaspoons of ground or crushed seeds to 1 cup of water. Boil briefly, then cover and steep for 10 minutes. Strain.

Catnip *(Nepeta cataria)*

Sometimes called Catmint, Catnep, Catrup, Catswort, Field Balm, and Nip, this herb, as we all know, is irresistible to cats. They will search it out, roll over and over in it, and ecstatically spread it everywhere. A member of the mint family, catnip, when brewed in tea, is thought to relieve upset stomachs, bronchitis, colic, spasms, flatulence, and acidity. It has also been used to treat hysteria, nervousness, and headaches, and as an enema. Originally native to Europe, catnip is now found wild in many parts of the United States.

PLANT: Perennial, hardy to − 30°F (− 34°C). Its erect, square, branching stem is hairy, with pointed scalloped leaves that have gray or whitish hairs on the lower side. Flowers are white with purple spots, and grow in spikes from June to September. The plant's odor is mint-like, bitter, and pungent.

HEIGHT: 2 to 3 feet.

SOIL: Moist, rich.

EXPOSURE: Sun or partial shade.

PROPAGATION: Sow seeds ¼ inch deep in spring or fall, during the third lunar phase. Plants will self-sow. They can also be reproduced by root cuttings, stem cuttings, and layering.

CARE: Thin plants to 12 inches apart. They tend to become scraggly, so cut back after they flower to keep them looking neat, and to prevent them from spreading. If there are cats

around, you'll want to protect young seedlings until they are large enough to resist damage by enthusiastic felines who roll in and eat them. It's said cats won't trouble a seeded bed, but *will* go for transplanted seedlings. Most growers, however, maintain that *their* cats don't seem to sense the distinction and get to the catnip no matter how it has been planted. Cultivated near eggplant, tomatoes, turnips, and/or radishes, catnip is said to discourage the flea beetles that attack these plants.

PART USED FOR TEA: Leaves.

TASTE: Aromatic, minty.

CAUTION: There has been talk in some quarters that catnip tea should be drunk sparingly. At least one medicinal-plant expert believes that catnip contains a hallucinogenic substance that affects humans as well as cats. The Food and Drug Administration, however, does not include catnip on its "hit list."

How to brew

BY INFUSION: Use 1 teaspoon of dried herb, or 3 teaspoons of fresh herb, with 1 cup of boiling water. Make sure the mixture is steeped only and not allowed to boil.

Chamomile *(Anthemis nobilis)*

Other names for *Anthemis nobilis* include Roman Chamomile, Garden Chamomile, Ground Apple, Low Chamomile, Whig Plant, Manzanilla, and Maythen. Roman or English chamomile is the plant most often used in herb gardens. It is the emblem of the sweetness of humility. Pronounced "kamomeel," the word *chamomile* comes from the Greek *kamai*, meaning "on the ground," and *melon*, meaning "apple," for ground apple. The Spanish word, *manzanilla*, also means "little apple." When bruised or walked on, chamomile produces a delightful apple-like odor, making it one of the oldest favorites among herbs. Shakespeare's Falstaff said of it, "The more it is trodden on, the faster it grows, yet youth the more it is wasted, the sooner it wears." This, perhaps, derives from the ancient Egyptian belief that chamomile prevented aging. Tea prepared from the flowers is thought to be a moderate sedative. It is also soothing for indigestion and good for flatulent colic, fever, and restlessness in children.

PLANT: Perennial, hardy to − 20°F (− 29°C). An evergreen, its aromatic leaves are light, bright green, and finely cut. Chamomile is found wild in dry fields and around gardens and cultivated grounds. The solitary terminal daisy-like flowerheads with their yellow, disc-like centers and silver-white petals, rise above the plant in June and July.

HEIGHT: 3 to 12 inches.

SOIL: Moist, well-drained soil.

EXPOSURE: Sun or partial shade.

PROPAGATION: By seeds or root division. Sow seeds ¼ inch deep in spring or fall during the third lunar phase. The seeds, however, are slow to germinate. You can also take root divisions or rooted pieces off established plants and replant these.

CARE: Plants should be 6 inches apart, in a clean, weed-free area. Chamomile is a creeping herb, and the stems root themselves as they spread. When mowed, chamomile makes a good lawn substitute. It can also be used as a ground cover. In regions with dry, hot summers, it dies and must be established again by replanting.

PART USED FOR TEA: Flowers.

TASTE: Light, apple-like.

How to brew

BY INFUSION: 1 tablespoon of fresh flowers or 2 teaspoons of dried flowers to 1 cup of boiling water. Steep for ½ hour or to taste.

Chrysanthemum *(Chrysanthemum species)*

The name *chrysanthemum* comes from the Greek words *chrysos*, meaning "gold," and *anthos*, meaning "flower." Native to China, the original wild, delicate white or yellow blossoms were about the size of a dime before hybridization and selective cultivation made possible the many showy varieties we associate with the plant today. Cultivation of the chrysanthemum began more than 2,000 years ago in China, where it is considered the flower of immortality. Tea made from dried flowers was served to Chinese emperors, and today the best grade tea flowers go for as much as $30 a pound. The chrysanthemum is also the imperial emblem of Japan. The flower was not introduced into Europe until the middle of the eighteenth century. It was brought to America in 1798. The Chinese and Japanese cultivated the perennial varieties, and it is these that are used for tea.

PLANT: Perennial. The plant has erect, usually highly branched stems. Leaves are alternate, lobed, and toothed— or sometimes smooth-edged. Flowers appear on stem ends in late summer and consist of many florets, some of which are disc florets like those that compose the eyes of daisies. These are generally encircled by a row of toothed or toothless petal-like ray florets. The fruits are hard and one-seeded.

HEIGHT: From less than 1 foot to 5 feet, depending on variety.

SOIL: Sandy, well-drained, rich.

EXPOSURE: Full or partial sun.

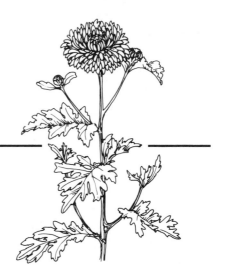

PROPAGATION: Sow seed indoors, and place seedlings outside when danger of frost has passed. Root divisions in spring. Also cuttings taken in fall and rooted indoors for outdoor planting in spring. The soil around roots should be firm.

CARE: Space plants from 1 foot apart to 3 feet or more, depending on the variety. The usual hardy "mum" for garden cultivation should be kept pinched back to about 6 inches until the middle or end of July. This promotes bushiness and flowering. Also, watch out for nematodes. Plant marigolds near the mums; a chemical exuded from marigold roots keeps nematodes away. Cut the plants down to 9 inches after they have flowered. Fertilize with manure from time to time.

PART USED FOR TEA: Flowers. For a sweet tea, use only petals.

TASTE: Tangy, aromatic, similar to the taste of artichoke hearts. Sweeten with honey or sugar.

How to brew

BY INFUSION: Cover 2 teaspoons of dried petals, or 3 teaspoons of fresh petals, with 1 cup of boiling water. Cover, and steep to taste.

Cicely *(Myrrhis odorata)*

Pronounced like "Sicily," this herb goes by other names as well: Sweet Cicely, Myrrh Flower, Sweet Chervil, Anise Fern, and Shepherd's Needle. Throughout Europe, cicely is found in hedges, on the edges of woods, and on mountainsides. Its botanical name, *Myrrhis*, comes from the Greek and means "perfume." However, though the plant is strongly scented, there is no recorded history of its being used for its scent. Old herbals do mention that cicely leaves can enhance a salad. Medicinally, it is believed to be a general tonic and appetite stimulant, and is considered mildly laxative. It is also believed helpful in treating coughs. In ancient times, a root decoction boiled in wine was administered in case of bites by poisonous snakes, spiders, and mad dogs.

PLANT: Hardy perennial, to − 20°F (− 29°C). The long, thick roots send up lacy, delicate, green leaves with finely cut pairs of leaflets resembling those of a fern or tansy. White flowers, which appear in late May and early June, are followed by dark brown seeds about 1 inch long.

HEIGHT: 2 to 3 feet.

SOIL: Rich, moist, well-drained.

EXPOSURE: Shade or partial shade.

PROPAGATION: Seeds planted in autumn during the third lunar phase, while they are still fresh. The seeds take up to 8

months to germinate, producing seedlings by the following spring. The plant self-sows freely. Roots of mature plants can be divided in fall or early spring.

CARE: Transplant seedlings to their permanent positions in spring, spacing them 2 feet apart. Cicely is a good plant for a shady flower garden.

PART USED FOR TEA: Leaves.

TASTE: Sweet, anise-like.

How to brew

BY INFUSION: 1 teaspoon of dried leaves, or 3 teaspoons of fresh leaves, to 1 cup of boiling water. Steep to taste.

Clover *(Trifolium pratense)*

Clover goes by many other names: Red Clover, Wild Clover, Broad-leafed Clover, and Purple Clover. In ancient times, it was believed that those who carried a triple-leaf clover should be able to detect witches, sorcerers, and good fairies. Christians thought the three-part leaf a symbol of the Trinity and designed many of their churches and church windows in that shape. The blossoms are believed to be a cough remedy. The tea is also believed to stimulate the liver and gall bladder, and people with constipation or a sluggish appetite have been advised to take it in some cases. Children pluck the blossoms and suck the sweet juice out of them, and in Shakespeare's time the flowers were called "honey stalks" because they were liked so much by bees. Clover is found throughout meadows all over North America and Europe.

PLANT: Short-lived perennial, regarded as an annual or a biennial as a result. The trifoliate leaves spring upward from the root on long reddish stems covered with close-pressed whitish hairs. Pink, purple, or red flowerheads bloom in July and August.

HEIGHT: To 2 feet.

SOIL: Moderate fertility. Neutral or alkaline.

EXPOSURE: Sun.

PROPAGATION: By seeds sown in spring, or in late summer and fall for the following spring. Clover is often used as a

cover crop by farmers, so seeds can usually be found through farm seed-supply stores.

CARE: Space 8 inches apart. Easy care; thrives in common garden soil. Good in rock gardens.

PART USED FOR TEA: Blossoms, usually dried. Air-drying rather than oven-drying is recommended.

TASTE: Delicate, sweet.

How to brew

BY INFUSION: Add 1 teaspoonful of the dried flowering tops, cut small, to 1 cup of boiling water. Steep to taste. Clover tea is good with some dried rose hips, lemon, wild mint, or, of course, clover honey.

Coltsfoot *(Tussilago farfara)*

Common names for this herb include British Tobacco, Bullsfoot, Butterbur, Coughwort, Flower Velure, Foal's Foot, Horse Foot, Horse Hoof, Bull's Foot, Ginger Root, Donnhove, and Filius Ante Patrem. Native to Europe and Asia, but naturalized elsewhere, including the United States, coltsfoot is found in pastures, along stream banks, and on embankments. In the eighteenth century, coltsfoot pancakes were a popular delicacy, particularly on Shrove Tuesday. A few tablespoons of dried leaves were soaked in water for about 5 minutes, drained, and added to the pancake batter. Coltsfoot tea is believed to be a cough remedy and to relieve cases of bronchial catarrh, hoarseness, and clogged breathing passages. Herbalists as far back as Pliny and Dioscorides regarded it as the best herb for lung and thoracic complaints. In times of tobacco shortages, it was also smoked. The herb is rich in calcium, potassium, sulfur, and vitamin C.

PLANT: Perennial. Bright yellow flowers appear on scaly, bare stalks. When the flowers have bloomed, the plant sends up long-stemmed, hoof-shaped, serrated leaves, which are woolly white on the underside. This unusual growing pattern gave coltsfoot its Latin name, *filius ante patrem*, or "son before father."

HEIGHT: Less than 1 foot.

SOIL: Damp, limy.

EXPOSURE: Full sun.

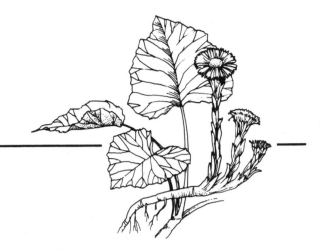

PROPAGATION: Seeds planted during the third lunar phase, or by root division.

CARE: Space mature plants 6 to 8 inches apart, but watch them, or they'll spread widely.

PART USED FOR TEA: Leaves and flowers.

TASTE: Fragrant, strong, somewhat like sweet potatoes.

How to brew

LEAVES OR FLOWERS, BY INFUSION: Blossoms should be collected as soon as they open, leaves when they reach full size. Use 1 teaspoon of dried, or 3 teaspoons of fresh, leaves or flowers. Steep them in boiling water for 30 minutes. The tea is especially good when brewed with horehound or marshmallow.

LEAVES, BY DECOCTION: For colds and asthma, 1 ounce of dried leaves in 1 quart of water, boiled down to 1 pint. Strain, and sweeten with honey.

Comfrey *(Symphytum officinale)*

Some common names for this plant are Healing Herb, Blackwort, Knitbone, Wallwort, Knitback, Consound, Ass Ear, Yalluc, Boneset, Gum Plant, Bruisewort, Slippery Root, Salsify, and Common Comfrey. In the Middle Ages, comfrey was used mainly as a poultice believed to heal—hence its names "boneset" and "bruisewort." The Crusaders believed it would repair broken bones and battered bodies. A rootstock decoction is believed to make good gargle for hoarseness, inflammation of the throat, and bleeding gums. As a tea, it is also considered beneficial for digestive and stomach problems, excessive menstrual flow, and intestinal difficulties.

PLANT: Perennial. Hardy to −40°F (−40°C). The juicy root is black outside, fleshy and white inside, and often grows to 1 foot in length and 1 inch in diameter. The stem is hollow, angular, and hairy. Large, oblong lower leaves—up to 10 inches long—resemble a donkey's ears, giving the plant one common name: "ass ear." Leaves get smaller the higher up on the plant they are. White, pink, or pale purple bell-like flowers hang in clusters, appearing in April or May, and continuing to flower until the first frost. The plant has a medicinal smell.

HEIGHT: To 3 feet.

SOIL: Moist, any type.

EXPOSURE: Sun or partial shade.

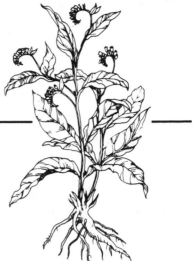

CAUTION: The use of comfrey is currently controversial among herbalists. Some maintain that it can be safely consumed; others contend that it is carcinogenic.

PROPAGATION: By seed planted in fall during the third or fourth lunar phase, or by root division. It is a difficult plant to eradicate; like horseradish, its roots produce new plants from any sliver left in the ground.

CARE: Water regularly. Space 3 feet apart, and keep weeded.

PART USED FOR TEA: Roots and leaves.

TASTE: Slightly bitter. Lemon balm, apple mint, or honey are usually used to sweeten.

How to brew

ROOTS OR LEAVES, BY INFUSION: Use 2 teaspoons of ground or crushed rootstock in ½ cup of boiling water, or 1 teaspoon dried (3 teaspoons fresh) leaves in 1 cup of boiling water. Steep to taste. The roots can also be brewed with an equal part of dandelion root to make an herbal "coffee."

ROOTS, BY DECOCTION: Boil 2 teaspoons of crushed or ground rootstock in 1 cup of water.

Dandelion *(Taraxacum officinale)*

Other popular names for this widespread plant are Priest's Crown, Swine's Snout, Blowball, Cankerwort, Lion's Tooth, White Endive, Dent-de-Lion, Wet-a-Bed. Considered a weed by farmers and gardeners, it is found throughout the Northern Hemisphere, growing in meadows, fields, ditches, and the most fastidious gardener's lawn. The name *dandelion* arose from the plant's deeply incised leaves. In French, *dent de lion* means "lion's tooth." Dandelion tea is said to help prevent and expel kidney stones, and it is also taken to stimulate liver and gall-bladder activity. The root is believed to affect all forms of secretion and excretion from the body, removing poisons, and acting as a tonic and stimulant as well. Dandelion tea is also believed to alleviate rheumatism.

PLANT: Perennial. The stake-like, milky root bores deep into the earth. Serrated leaves grow in a rosette from this taproot. In spring and fall one or more hollow naked flower stems culminate in a single composite golden flowerhead. The familiar puffball of seeds outfitted with fuzzy white parachute tufts are the delight of children, who watch them soar in all directions when they blow on them.

HEIGHT: Less than 1 foot.

SOIL: Dry or wet, poor or rich (to the gardener's dismay).

EXPOSURE: Sun, partial shade, or shade.

PROPAGATION: Seed. In some areas, dandelions are specially cultivated for the roots or salad greens. But most of us know a

nearby field or garden where they can be had for the asking.
If you're growing dandelions wittingly, however, you may
want to plant them in rows (as they are planted when
cultivated), so you can keep them weeded. This is a most
rewarding plant to *try* to grow, since failure is almost
impossible.

PART USED FOR TEA: Leaves and root. The leaves should be
gathered when young and tender.

TASTE: The leaf has a robust, grassy aroma and a bland taste.
It is good when blended with mint, or when served cold.
The root is bitter, with a coffee-like taste. Roasted and mixed
with ground chicory, it is sometimes used as a caffeine-free
coffee substitute.

How to brew

LEAVES, BY INFUSION: Steep 1 teaspoon of dried, or 3
teaspoons of fresh, leaves in 1 cup of boiling water. Or take
2 teaspoons of leaves and root, and steep to taste in 1 cup of
boiling water.

ROOTS, BY DECOCTION: 4 ounces of fresh root or 1 ounce of
dried root bruised or ground, and placed in 2 pints of water.
Boil down to 1 pint, and strain.

Dill *(Anethum graveolens)*

Dill, whose other names are Dillweed, Dilly, and Garden Dill, received its name from the Norse word *dilla*, which means "to lull." Magicians used it to cast and ward off spells. It was called the "meeting-house seed" by American colonists, who nibbled it to prevent hunger while they spent long hours in church. During the Middle Ages, a bit of dill drunk in wine was believed to enhance passion. Dill tea is a popular remedy for an upset stomach, and it is also used to stimulate the appetite. A decoction of the seed is said to overcome insomnia and pains caused by flatulence. Chewing the seeds is thought to get rid of halitosis. Native to western Asia, dill now grows weedily in the grain fields of Spain, Portugal, and Italy.

PLANT: A hardy annual, sometimes classed as a biennial. Its single round stalk has shiny green feathery leaves, and dill is often confused with fennel, though dill's spindly taproot is not usable. Fennel commonly shows many stems from a single root, but dill seldom has more than one. Numerous yellow flowers bloom in flat terminal umbrella-shaped clusters which appear from July to September. Seeds follow.

HEIGHT: 3 to 4 feet.

SOIL: Average, well-drained.

EXPOSURE: Sun. Keep out of wind so seeds won't disperse prematurely and plants won't bend to the ground.

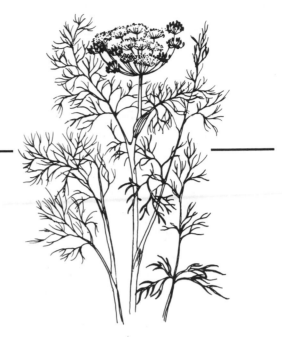

PROPAGATION: By seed sown ¼ inch deep in spring or fall during the first or second lunar phase.

CARE: When seedlings are about 2 inches high, thin them so the plants stand about 12 inches apart. If growth seems weak when the plants are 1 foot tall, fertilize with an all-purpose mixture.

PART USED FOR TEA: Leaves gathered early in summer or seed gathered in late summer and early fall.

TASTE: Seed tea—sharp, pungent; leaf tea—milder.

How to brew

SEEDS, BY INFUSION: Steep 2 teaspoons of crushed seeds in 1 cup of boiling water for 10 to 15 minutes.

LEAVES, BY INFUSION: Add 1 teaspoon of dried, or 3 teaspoons of crushed fresh, leaves to 1 cup of boiling water. Steep to taste.

Elder *(Sambucus nigra)*

Common names for this herb include Blackberried European Elder, Boor Tree, Ellanwood, European Elder, Black Elder, Bountry, Ellhorn, and German Elder. In the past, this shrub or tree was regarded as magical and was believed to dispel demons. Undertakers once carried pieces of elder to protect them against the numerous spirits they might encounter in the course of their work. In Europe, men doffed their hats in the tree's presence and offered prayers to the elder "mother" before gathering her berries. Christians believed elder to be the wood of the Cross. Its honey-scented flowers were considered sacred to the Scandinavian goddess of love, Hulda. In the early herbals, hot elder tea was listed as a mild stimulant, dispelling colds, catarrh, and flatulence, and promoting perspiration. When served cold, it was considered a diuretic. The North American Elder, widespread in the United States, is similar in appearance and properties.

PLANT: Perennial. A shrub or small tree, it is found wild in Europe in moist, shady places. The bark is light brown near the bottom of the stems, gray-white and warty higher up. The leaves are composed of several pairs of oval, opposite dark green, and finely serrated leaflets. White to yellow-white flower clusters appear in June and July, developing into green berries that subsequently turn red-brown, then shiny black.

HEIGHT: 10 to 30 feet.

SOIL: Fertile, damp.

EXPOSURE: Sun or partial shade.

PROPAGATION: By cuttings, root division, or seeds planted during the third lunar phase.

CARE: Rampant and fast growing, the elder can become wild looking if not pruned every dormant season to keep it dense and shrubby. New growths sprout readily from the stumps.

PART USED FOR TEA: Flowerheads.

TASTE: Sweet, honey flavored. Often combined with *Thea sinensis*, peppermint, yarrow, or other herbs.

How to brew

BY INFUSION: Add 2 tablespoons of flowers to 1 cup of boiling water. Steep to taste.

Fennel *(Foeniculum vulgare)*

Common names for Fennel are Wild Fennel, Sweet Fennel, Fenkel, and Large Fennel. Fennel grows wild in the Mediterranean area and in Asia Minor, but is extensively naturalized and cultivated in the United States. Like its close cousin dill, it was also used in medicine and sorcery, and it was mentioned frequently by Pliny. Both the seed and root are considered excellent stomach and intestinal remedies. Fennel is believed to arouse appetite, to relieve spasms, flatulence, colic, and abdominal cramps, and to expel mucous accumulations. The seeds have been a symbol of heroism. Seed tea boiled in barley water is thought to stimulate the flow of milk in nursing mothers.

PLANT: Perennial, but most gardeners grow it as an annual or biennial. The leaves are feathery and grow on hollow, fleshy stems. Flat umbels of yellow flowers grow at the ends of stems that rise above the foliage. The *vulgare* variety is grown for its seeds and leaves. Others are grown for their roots (*finocchio*) or stems (*carosella*).

HEIGHT: To 5 feet.

SOIL: Light, well-drained, good garden soil, preferably lime-rich.

EXPOSURE: Full sun.

PROPAGATION: Seeds sown in spring during the third lunar phase for a fall seed harvest. Also, by root division.

CARE: Thin seedlings to about 1 foot apart. Fennel does not transplant easily. Tall plants must be sheltered from the wind or staked when 18 inches tall.

PART USED FOR TEA: Seeds, picked before they scatter at the touch. Also, leaves picked before the plants have blossomed.

TASTE: Delightful, reminiscent of anise, peppermint, and licorice.

How to brew

LEAVES, BY INFUSION: Pour 1 cup of boiling water over 2 teaspoons of dried leaves or 3 teaspoons of fresh leaves. Steep to taste.

SEEDS, BY DECOCTION: Crush 1 tablespoon of seeds, and add to 2 cups of boiling water. Reduce temperature, and allow mixture to simmer gently for 5 to 10 minutes.

Fenugreek *(Trigonella foenum–graecum)*

Also called Bird's Foot or Greek Hay-Seed, this herb is one of the oldest-known medicinal plants. Its use dates back to the ancient Egyptians and Greeks. It was believed to strengthen those recovering from an illness or suffering from tuberculosis, and it was also taken for bronchitis, colds, or fevers. Some consider it an aphrodisiac. The Indians call the fenugreek leaf *methi* and use it in their cooking. Health-food enthusiasts find the seeds excellent for sprouting. And, in Greece, the seeds are boiled and eaten with honey. Fenugreek is believed to give strength to pregnant women and to increase lactation. The seeds of this legume are plentiful: each pod contains sixteen of them.

PLANT: Annual. A long taproot sends up a round stem. The plant resembles an almost-branchless sweet clover with triple leaves. Yellow, richly scented, pear-shaped flowers appear in June and July, followed by the sixteen-seeded, compressed legume, which looks like an elongated string bean. The seeds are very rich in minerals. In chemical composition, they are close to cod liver oil.

HEIGHT: 15 to 18 inches.

SOIL: Sandy, dry.

EXPOSURE: Direct sunlight.

PROPAGATION: By seeds planted during the first or second lunar phase.

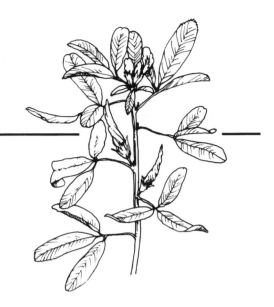

CARE: Space plants 4 inches apart. Dig soil deeply, and make sure it is kept well drained and weeded.

PART USED FOR TEA: Seeds or leaves.

TASTE: Pleasant, bitter, reminiscent of maple and vanilla.

How to brew

LEAVES, BY INFUSION: Cover 1 teaspoon dried, or 3 teaspoons fresh crushed leaves with 1 cup of boiling water. Allow to steep. Drink by itself or with other herbs such as alfalfa or one of the mints.

SEEDS, BY DECOCTION: 1 teaspoonful of seeds to 1 cup of boiling water, boiled until the seeds are tender. For extra nutrition, don't strain the tea, and eat the seeds. This tea is very good with honey or lemon.

Flax *(Linum usitatissimum)*

Flax also goes by the names Linseed, Common Flax, Mary's Linen Cloth, Flax Seed, and Lint Bells. The source of linen, flax is native to all Mediterranean countries and is widely cultivated in the United States and Canada. It is also found wild along roadsides and in waste places. The crushed seed is often used in granola-like cereals and breads; the seeds are quite high in nutrition. Flax seeds have been considered effective in treating coughs, catarrh, and lung and chest problems, as well as digestive and urinary disorders. In the past, the fresh herb was applied as a poultice for rheumatic pains and for softening hard swellings. An ailing baby would sometimes be laid upon the ground in a flax field and sprinkled with flax seeds. The seeds were then planted where the baby had lain, and it was believed he or she would recover as the seeds sprouted.

PLANT: Annual. The erect, willowy stems are blue-green, with few branches and simple, alternate, oblong leaves. From June to August, each branch has one or two blue or blue-violet five-petaled flowers. The smooth, flattened, shiny light brown seeds are borne in an eight- to ten-seeded capsule.

HEIGHT: 1 to 2 feet.

SOIL: Well-drained alkaline soil, made porous by gravel and rocks.

EXPOSURE: Full sun.

PROPAGATION: By seeds sown in the spring during the first or second lunar phase. Sow where the plants are to grow. They will germinate in 8 days.

CARE: Space mature plants 12 inches apart. Flax planted near potatoes helps discourage potato bugs.

PART USED FOR TEA: Seed.

TASTE: Soothing, gelatinous.

CAUTION: Seeds that are going to be brewed should be thoroughly ripe and should be soaked overnight in water that is then discarded. Immature seed contains some irritant properties and can cause poisoning.

How to brew

BY DECOCTION: Crush or grind 1 tablespoon of the seed, and boil in 1 quart of water until ½ quart remains. Strain. Add honey and molasses to taste.

Fraxinella *(Dictamnus albus)*

Also called Gas Plant, Bastard Dittany, Burning Bush, Diptam, Dittany, False Dittany, and White Dittany. Fraxinella is native to Europe and Asia and is found as far eastward as China. It is sometimes cultivated as a garden ornamental in the northern United States. The volatile, scented oil of the flowers gives off a vapor on summer evenings, and if a match is lit nearby, the vapor will flash. A decoction of the root is believed to relieve fever and stomach cramps, and a decoction of the root and seed is used to treat kidney and bladder stones, to bring on menstruation, and to alleviate hysteria. Tea brewed from the root, leaves, or seed was popular with the American colonists.

PLANT: Perennial. A knobby, whitish root sends up round, downy, green and purple stems. The leaflets of dark green, shiny compound leaves are alternate, oval, and covered with glandular dots. The large, showy, rose, white, or red-purple flowers appear in June and July.

HEIGHT: 3 feet.

SOIL: Moderately rich, somewhat light soil, deeply dug.

EXPOSURE: Sun or partial shade.

PROPAGATION: Newly ripe seeds planted 1 inch deep in fall during the third or fourth lunar phase. The following spring, seedlings will appear. Also can be propagated by 3-inch root cuttings in spring, although this is usually not as successful.

CARE: Keep seedlings well weeded. When they are 2 years old, they may be transplanted. Flowers will not appear until the fourth year.

PART USED FOR TEA: Root, leaves, seed.

TASTE: The white-flowered variety has a lemony fragrance and taste. The pink-flowered variety is less lemony but has an added taste of almond and vanilla.

CAUTION: Contact with the fraxinella plant can cause skin irritation if the skin is exposed to sunlight after contact.

How to brew

LEAVES, BY INFUSION: The leaves are best when dried, using 1 teaspoon of dried leaf to 1 cup of boiling water. Steep to taste. Refreshing.

SEEDS OR ROOTS, BY DECOCTION: Use 1 tablespoon of crushed or powdered seed or root to 2 cups of water. Boil down to 1 cup. This method produces a more medicinal tea.

Geranium *(Pelargonium* species)

Scented geraniums of the genus *Pelargonium*, also called Stork's Bill, were first brought to England from the Cape of Good Hope around 1632. By the late 1700s, Dutch and English navigators had imported countless varieties for enthusiastic gardeners. Shortly after 1795, the French discovered that oil from some varieties of rose-scented geraniums could be used as a less expensive substitute for attar of roses in perfume making. To this day, rose geraniums are grown in large amounts for this purpose—approximately 1 pound of leaves produces 1 gram of oil. Not much has been written about the medicinal qualities of the pelargoniums, whose name means "stork's bill" and derives from their elongated seed cases. Most have astringent properties. One herbal says they are valuable in treating dysentery and stomach and intestinal ulcers.

PLANT: Very tender perennial. The basic scented geranium is the rose geranium, a large plant with deeply cut gray-green leaves, lavender flowers, and a rose-like fragrance. Others of the more than eighty varieties of pelargonium have their own distinctive leaf shape, scent, and blossoms.

HEIGHT: Varies according to variety and where grown. In temperate climates they can reach 5 feet.

SOIL: Well-drained, loose soil.

EXPOSURE: Sun or partial sun.

PROPAGATION: By cuttings cut straight across the stem and placed in clean, sharp sand. Water sparingly until good green growth shows. Plant outdoors in late spring or early summer when danger of frost has passed. Also can be grown from seed.

CARE: Plant scented geraniums 36 inches apart. Be sure they're brought indoors well before the first frost. (See additional information on care in chapter 3.) They can also be grown in pots or tubs. Geraniums are insect resistant, and white-flower varieties are said to attract Japanese beetles, which eat the flower and die before doing any further damage.

PART USED FOR TEA: Leaves.

TASTE: Depends on variety within the family, each of which has its own taste and scent. Favorites are apricot, strawberry, apple, rose, peach, lime, lemon, orange, nutmeg, almond, licorice, and coconut.

How to brew

BY INFUSION: Fresh leaves have more flavor, but most varieties dry well, too. Use 1 teaspoon of dried leaves, or 3 teaspoons of crushed, fresh leaves, in 1 cup of boiling water. Steep to taste, and enjoy.

Ginseng *(Panax quinquefolium)*

Other names for this plant are American Ginseng, Tartar Root, Man's Health, Ninsin, Five Fingers, Seng, Five-leafed Ginseng, and Redberry. American Ginseng is occasionally found wild in the rich, cool woodlands of North America. It was prevalent there until it was decimated by avid hunters of the sought-after root. Much ginseng is now grown under cultivation in Wisconsin. Ginseng is a plant of mystery and superstition, evoking legends of fortunes made and lost overnight. Since before 3000 B.C., the Chinese have valued the root as a cure-all. They have used extracts as a general tonic, curative, strength builder, and—most importantly —an aphrodisiac and sexual rejuvenator. Initially, only the emperor, his household, and his favored friends were allowed to use this herb. The name ginseng comes from the Chinese *jen shen*, meaning "man-root," and derives from the root's resemblance to the human shape.

PLANT: Perennial. The aromatic root can grow to a length of 2 feet or more and is often divided at the end. At the top of a simple stem are five oblong, finely serrated leaflets. A solitary umbrella-shaped cluster of greenish-yellow flowers appears from June to August, followed by small, red, edible berries.

HEIGHT: Less than 1 foot.

SOIL: Rich, loamy, well-drained, under forest trees or a wooden lath frame, constructed over the planting area to protect the herb from direct sunlight.

EXPOSURE: Shade.

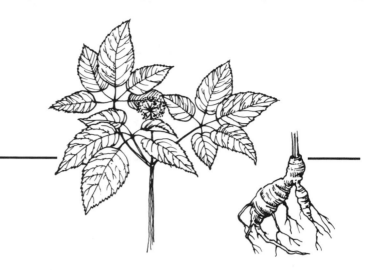

PROPAGATION: By seed, planted during the third or fourth lunar phase, seedlings, or rootstock. Ginseng requires from 5 to 7 years to mature from seed, 3 to 4 from roots.

CARE: Roots can be planted between October and April, 2 inches deep, and 8 inches apart. Cultivation is difficult. Gardeners should seek complete growing information when they obtain seeds or roots.

PART USED FOR TEA: Root, usually dug in fall.

TASTE: Parsnip-like. Bland; sweeten with honey or sugar.

How to brew

Place ginseng root (most are 4 to 6 inches long) and 1 quart of water into a closed glass or earthenware (*not* metal) container. Place this container into another pot that is also filled with water, and boil the root slowly for 2 to 3 hours, until the water in the outer ginseng pot has been reduced by half. Strain and drink immediately. Do not store the tea for more than a day, as it loses its potency. Use the root several times until you feel it has lost its power. Then place it in a jar of honey for several weeks until you have ginseng honey and a candied root you can chew on, for the last bit of flavor.

Goldenrod (*Solidago odora*)

This plant is also known as Blue Mountain Tea, Sweet-scented Goldenrod, Anise-scented Goldenrod, Bohea-tea, and Wound Weed. More than eighty species of goldenrod are found in the United States, and while several (including *S. virgaurea* and *S. canadensis*) make good tea, it is *Solidago odora* that sacrifices the showiness of the other goldenrods' blossoms for its strong scent, making it both tasty and fragrant. The botanical name *Solidago* comes from the Latin *solidus*, which means "whole," and *agere*, which means "to perform," a reference to the healing powers of the herb. American Indians made good use of these qualities: the Zuñis chewed the blossoms and slowly swallowed the astringent juice to alleviate sore throats; other tribes used infusions of flowers and leaves for fevers and chest pains. Early white settlers in North America believed goldenrod tea would relieve urinary obstructions and dropsy, and would stimulate perspiration.

PLANT: Hardy perennial. The creeping roots produce a simple, slender stem. The dark green leaves are thin, lance-shaped, and covered with transparent dots. The leaves have no stems. Golden-yellow flower spires appear on the ends of the stalks from July to September.

HEIGHT: 2 to 4 feet.

SOIL: Dry, sandy.

EXPOSURE: Full or partial sun.

PROPAGATION: Seeds planted during the third lunar phase. Also by root division. The plant self-sows readily, once it is established.

CARE: Space plants 1 foot apart. Goldenrod is easy to find by roadsides and similar environments, and it will transplant well if you choose blooming plants, cut them back, and carefully dig and replant them at that time. Give transplants more fertile soil than you found them in. Divide and replant every 2 or 3 years, so plants don't choke one another out. Soil that's too rich will stunt the plants. Remove faded flowers promptly to prevent too much self-seeding.

PART USED FOR TEA: Young leaves and fully opened flowers.

TASTE: Anise-like.

How to brew

BY INFUSION: Cover 1 heaping teaspoon of dry herb, or 3 teaspoons of fresh herb, with 1 cup of boiling water. Steep for at least 10 minutes. Strain and sweeten to taste.

Hawthorn (*Crataegus* species)

Hawthorn's other names include Mayblossom and Thornapple. A symbol of hope, the hawthorn shrub or tree is considered sacred by some, and it is believed to have formed Christ's crown of thorns. The botanical name comes from the Greek word *kratos*, which means "strong," and was given because of the hardness of hawthorn wood. The Pilgrims' ship *Mayflower* was named for this herb. Hawthorn has always been especially regarded as a heart tonic, and its value is now under medical investigation, particularly in regard to its old reputation as a reliever of angina pectoris and abnormal heart action. Hawthorn has also been considered an artery softener, helpful in treating arteriosclerosis. Early American settlers used the tea to relieve kidney ailments and nervous conditions, including insomnia, giddiness, and stress.

PLANT: Perennial. It grows as either a shrub or small tree. Its sharp 1- to 5-inch thorns have made it a favorite hedgerow in England and Europe; the flowers and fruit must be harvested with care because of them. The trunk or stems are spiny, with hard, smooth, ash-gray bark. The small, dark green leaves are light bluish-green on the underside and have three irregularly toothed lobes. White flowers with round petals appear in clusters during May and June. The egg-shaped berry, or haw, that follows is a two- or three-seeded pome (the hawthorn is a close relative of the apple), scarlet on the outside, yellowish and pulpy inside.

HEIGHT: 3 to 15 feet.

SOIL: Any well-drained soil, with good lime content.

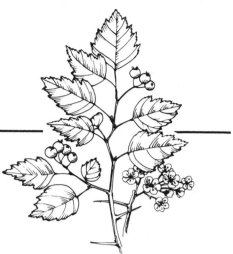

EXPOSURE: Full or partial sun.

PROPAGATION: Seed planted indoors in spring or in fall during the third lunar phase. Slow to germinate. Also stem cuttings.

CARE: If you're growing hawthorn as a tree, remove suckers from the trunk and around the base. If you're growing it as a hedge, space plants 3 feet apart, and keep them trimmed. Prune after the hawthorn has flowered. The deciduous hawthorn requires little care, having a naturally dense growth. However, sometimes the tops become *too* dense, and an annual thinning will minimize the danger of the plant's being uprooted by wind.

PART USED FOR TEA: Flowers, berries.

TASTE: Flowers are sweet-scented and bland. The berries are tart and fruity (similar to a crab apple).

How to brew

FLOWERS, BY INFUSION: Steep 2 teaspoons of herb in 1 cup of boiling water.

FRUITS, BY DECOCTION: Use 2 teaspoons of crushed fruit with 1 cup cold water. Let stand for 7 or 8 hours, then bring quickly to a boil and strain. Sweeten both teas with honey.

Hibiscus *(Abelmoschus moscheutos)*

Common names for this plant are Musk Seed Plant, Musk-mallow, and Target-leaved Hibiscus. Hibiscus flowers are a favorite for cooking purposes in Africa, the Far East, the Caribbean, and other tropical areas. Africans also make "karkade," a pleasant, tart beverage, by steeping 1 teaspoon of hibiscus flowers and 2 cloves in 1 cup of boiling water, then draining and adding honey to taste. Egyptians chew the seeds to relieve stomach problems, sweeten the breath, and soothe their nerves. They also consider hibiscus to have aphrodisiac powers.

PLANT: Annual or biennial. While it grows wild in tropical areas, it is not winter hardy and must be pot grown or protected in cold areas. Hibiscus stems bear alternate-lobed and irregularly toothed leaves, similar to those of a maple tree. Both sides of the leaf are thinly hairy. The large flowers are yellow with red centers. Kidney-shaped, grayish-brown seeds follow in oblong, hairy capsules that are up to 3 inches long.

HEIGHT: 2 to 6 feet.

SOIL: Loose, loamy soil, kept moist.

EXPOSURE: Full sun.

PROPAGATION: Seeds sown (indoors or outdoors, depending on weather zone) in January or February for flowers the same

year. In cold-weather areas place outdoors when danger of frost has passed.

CARE: Space plants 2 to 3 feet apart. Fertilize well. Mulch heavily in winter, or grow in pots and bring indoors. Prune in spring and fall as needed.

PART USED FOR TEA: Flowers.

TASTE: Tart and slightly lemony. The tea has a pale, ruby color.

How to brew

BY INFUSION: Measure 1 teaspoon of dried flowers or 3 teaspoons of fresh flowers. Cover with 1 cup of boiling water, and steep to taste. The longer you steep, the redder the tea will become. This brew is very good in combination with rose hips. Can be served hot or cold.

Hollyhock *(Alcea rosea)*

Common names for the Hollyhock are Althea Rose, Malva Flowers, Rose Mallow, Purple Malva. The flower of the hollyhock is cultivated for its beauty as well as its medicinal qualities. The plant is not known in the wild and is thought to have arisen in cultivation. The Egyptians used the leaves in cookery. Hollyhocks were brought to Europe at the time of the Crusades, and were cultivated in France by the Duke of Orléans, and in England by Lord Burlington. Tea made from the blossoms is believed to soothe inflammation of the mouth and throat, and a vapor bath of it is thought helpful for earaches. The tea is also said to be beneficial for chest complaints and an aid to digestion.

PLANT: Biennial. Both leaves and flowers cover the length of the tall, hairy unbranched stem. The 3- to 4-inch broad flowers appear from July to September and come in shades of red, purple, white, yellow, maroon, and salmon. They may have one or two sets of petals.

HEIGHT: Usually 5 to 6 feet tall, but can reach 15 feet.

SOIL: Deep, rich, well-drained.

EXPOSURE: Full or partial sun. Prefers a warm location sheltered from the wind.

PROPAGATION: Seeds planted during the third or fourth lunar phase germinate easily in about 5 days. Or, suckers can be taken from near the roots. Hollyhock self-seeds easily.

CARE: Space mature plants about 2 feet apart. If planted in unprotected spots, stalks should be supported. Plants propagated from self-seeding can be moved to a permanent place in spring. If not being grown as annuals, mound up soil around the plants to prevent winterkill.

PART USED FOR TEA: Flowers.

TASTE: The whole-flower tea can be tart and bitter. Petal tea, however, is tangy without bitterness, and most refreshing.

How to brew

BY INFUSION: 1 teaspoon of dried flowers or petals, or 3 teaspoons of fresh flowers or petals, to each cup of boiling water. Steep to taste.

Hop *(Humulus lupulus)*

The Hop, commonly named Northern Vine and Bine, has been used since the fourteenth century, chiefly to brew beer. Before then, people drank mead or ale beverages made from fermented honey or barley and flavored with ground ivy, yarrow, broom, wormwood, and other herbs. The hop grows wild in Europe and western Asia, and is cultivated in the United States. In Spanish the plant is called *Flores de Cerveza,* meaning "flowers of beer." The Romans ate young hop shoots like asparagus. The cones found on female plants are used to make beer, the pulp is used to make paper, and the fibers of the plant are made into linen. Female-flower hops tea is believed to induce sleep, improve the appetite, and aid against alcoholism. It is also recommended for nervous diarrhea, flatulence, and intestinal cramps. Hops' narcotic qualities are also considered a cure for uncontrolled sexual desires and a quarrelsome nature.

PLANT: Perennial. The vine, a twining climber, has a tough, flexible stem growing from a branched root. The three- to five-lobed, opposite, dark green leaves are heart shaped. Male flowers grow in loose bunches. The female flowers are small yellow-green cones (hops) that contain a resinous dust called lupulin, which gives the herb its distinctive taste and medicinal qualities.

HEIGHT: To 20 feet.

SOIL: Rich, loamy, well-watered.

EXPOSURE: Full sun or partial shade.

PROPAGATION: Seeds planted during the third lunar phase. They are not ordinarily carried by regular nurseries but can be found at seed companies that supply farmers. You can also purchase hop roots. Stem cuttings are successful once plants are established.

CARE: Space 2 feet apart. Keep sprouting seeds and roots well watered. The vine does well on trellises. Twining stems should be trained by hand in June and July. Cut stems to the ground after frost turns them brown.

PART USED FOR TEA: Female flowers (hops), leaves.

TASTE: Slightly peppery, yet mild. The tea is light yellow.

CAUTION: Because of lupulin's narcotic qualities, drink hops flower tea in moderation, and avoid prolonged use.

How to brew

LEAVES, BY INFUSION: 1 teaspoon dried leaves, or 3 teaspoons of fresh crushed leaves, in 1 cup of boiling water. Steep to taste.

FLOWERS, BY DECOCTION: Place 1 heaping tablespoon of hops flowers (cones) in ½ pint of cold water, bring to a simmer for 2 or 3 minutes. Steep well. Strain. Hops quickly lose their effectiveness when stored, so use them fresh.

Horehound (Marrubium vulgare)

Horehound is also called Hoarhound, Marrubium, and White Horehound, and ancient Egyptian priests called it the Seed of Horus, Bull's Blood, and Eye of the Star. Recommended in John Gerard's *Herball* of 1597 as an antidote for "those that drunk poyson or have been bitten of serpents," horehound tea is also suggested for pulmonary afflictions and as a useful standby for bronchitis, coughs, and colds. In Wales, infusions are used externally and internally to cure eczema and shingles. Because of its bitterness when unsweetened, horehound is sometimes thought to be marrob, one of the five bitter herbs mentioned in early writings as being eaten by Jews at Passover.

PLANT: Perennial. Supposedly hardy to − 30°F (− 34°C), but often subject to winterkill. Some gardeners treat it as a biennial. A fibrous, spindle-shaped root sends up bushy, square, downy stems. Aromatic, wrinkled, oval, gray-green leaves are tooth-edged and covered with white hair. A relative of mint, horehound has small creamy-white flowers from June to September.

HEIGHT: 1 to 3 feet.

SOIL: Sandy, not overly rich; dry and well-drained.

EXPOSURE: Sun.

PROPAGATION: By seeds planted during the third lunar phase. Germinates in 2 to 3 weeks. Also by root division or cuttings.

138

CARE: Plants should be placed 12 inches apart. Keep pinched back to prevent weediness, unless you want seeds —then let horehound go to bloom. In autumn, cut off old stalks.

PART USED FOR TEA: Leaves. Pick on a clear, dry day before the sun gets too hot and before blossoms have formed.

TASTE: Bittersweet, musky. Combines nicely with coltsfoot. Usually sweetened with honey or some ground ginger root.

How to brew

BY INFUSION: 1 teaspoon of dried leaves—or 3 teaspoons of fresh herb, crushed to release aromatic oils—to 1 cup of boiling water. Steep to taste.

Hyssop *(Hyssopus officinalis)*

Native to southern Europe and ranging eastward into central Asia, hyssop is also called the Sacred Herb. Its name is said to come from the Greek word *azob*, meaning "a holy herb," because it was used to clean temples and other sacred places. It is also said that ancient Egyptians and Hebrews used hyssop to cleanse lepers and that a prayer of King David was, "Purge me with hyssop, and I shall be clean." Some scholars believe hyssop was dipped in the lamb's blood that marked the doorposts on Passover eve. Others, however, think that a variety of marjoram or savory may have been used, rather than what we call hyssop today. Through the ages, hyssop has been a popular remedy for coughs, consumption, asthma, and pulmonary complaints. A decoction is supposed to fade black eyes and bruises, and hyssop tea is thought to calm the nerves and regulate blood pressure.

PLANT: Perennial, hardy to − 35°F (− 37°C). Similar to boxwood in appearance, hyssop's downy, woody stems sport small, narrow, pointed, dark green leaves. Rose-colored, white, or blue flowers grow in whorls at the tops of the branches and stems. They bloom from June to October.

HEIGHT: 1½ to 2 feet.

SOIL: Light, dry, well-drained. Preferably alkaline.

EXPOSURE: Full or partial sun in sheltered position.

PROPAGATION: By seeds sown in spring during the third lunar phase, or started indoors. Hyssop germinates readily but grows slowly. Also by root division in spring or fall.

CARE: If using as a hedge, space plants 12 inches apart. An almost-evergreen subshrub, hyssop can be trimmed like box, but it will not flower if the tops are cut off. So if you wish to replace plants that die, allow plants at the ends of the hedge to bloom and self-sow. Or you might place a couple of hyssop plants in a general planting area, 2 feet apart, and allow them to grow freely.

PART USED FOR TEA: Green tops of the herb—leaves, stems, and flowers.

TASTE: Bitter and minty, with a slight musky odor.

How to brew

BY INFUSION: Add 1 teaspoon dried hyssop tops and/or flowers to 1 covered cup of boiling water for 10 minutes, or longer to taste. Strain and sweeten with honey.

Jasmine *(Jasminum officinale)*

Sometimes called Poet's Jasmine, this vine-like plant with its captivating scent is native to warm parts of the Eastern Hemisphere. It can be grown outdoors in the southern United States, but must be taken indoors in winter in cold-weather areas. The name is derived from the Persian *yasmin*, and the summer jasmine of our gardens is a species native to Persia and northern India. When it was introduced to Europe in the mid-sixteenth century, it was grafted onto a hardier Spanish variety. Many think the scent of jasmine arouses erotic instincts, and a few drops of jasmine oil massaged on the body along with almond oil are believed to overcome frigidity. The essential oil of jasmine is used in the perfume industry, and the herb is grown extensively near Cannes and Grasse in the south of France. In India, jasmine is believed a remedy for snakebite. An infusion of the leaves is thought to alleviate eye problems.

PLANT: Tender perennial. A vine-like semi-evergreen plant, jasmine has many dark green leaflets arranged in opposite rows along the stem. Clusters of richly scented white flowers bloom over a long period from June to September. The fruits are two-lobed berries containing two to four seeds.

HEIGHT: To 30 feet in warm climates.

SOIL: Moist, well-drained garden soil.

EXPOSURE: Sun or partial shade.

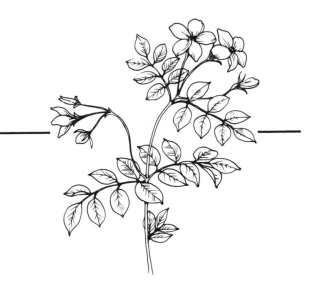

PROPAGATION: By stem cuttings of moderately firm shoots. Also by seeds and layering.

CARE: Planted outside in temperate climates, jasmine should be carefully trained against a wall or on a trellis. In colder climates, jasmine can be potted with a trellis support, and brought indoors in winter. No systematic annual pruning is required, but the plant is more likely to flourish if older, crowded stems are thinned out occasionally.

PART USED FOR TEA: Flowers.

TASTE: Fragrant, sweet.

How to brew

BY INFUSION: 1 teaspoon of dried flowers, or 3 teaspoons of fresh flowers, covered with 1 cup of boiling water and steeped to taste. Because of the euphoria aroused by jasmine's distinctive scent, it's hard to tell if it is the taste or the odor of this tea that makes it so delightful.

Juniper (*Juniperus communis*)

Juniper is also called Melmot Berries, Horse-Saver, and Bastard-Killer. Legend has it that it was a juniper bush that hid the infant Jesus from Herod's army. This is possible, since the strongly aromatic shrub is found in dry, rocky soil in Europe and Asia, as well as in North America from the Arctic Circle to Mexico. If you crush a juniper berry, you will smell the odor of gin and, indeed, the making of gin is the main commercial use of this herb. The word *gin* comes from the French word for juniper, *genièvre*. Juniper tea is said to relieve digestive problems resulting from an underproduction of hydrochloric acid, and it is also believed to be helpful for gastrointestinal infections, inflammations, and cramps. Juniper is also considered a diuretic.

PLANT: Perennial evergreen shrub with many very close branches. The bark is chocolate brown with red tinges. Needles have white stripes on top, and are shiny yellow-green underneath. From April to June, yellow male flowers occur in whorls on one plant, green female flowers on another. Green berry-like cones appear after the flowers, and it isn't until the second year that they ripen into bluish-black or dark purple fleshy fruit.

HEIGHT: 4 to 12 feet.

SOIL: Limestone, chalky.

EXPOSURE: Sunny.

PROPAGATION: By seed, but extremely slow; seeds won't germinate until the second or third year. A faster way is to

take cuttings in August, 4 to 6 inches long, stripped to 1 inch or so from the butt, and then place them in a shaded cold-frame bed of sand. They will be rooted by the following summer.

CARE: If you're planning to harvest the berries, keep pruning to a minimum, though you can trim a few straggly or lopsided branches by cutting tips of branches back to the first fork in spring. It's usually better to replace junipers when they've outgrown their space, rather than pruning them dramatically and sacrificing the berries and health of the shrub.

PART USED FOR TEA: Ripe female berries.

TASTE: Spicy, bittersweet, fragrant with an alpine-like tang, similar to that of gin.

How to brew

BY INFUSION: Steep 1 teaspoon of dried, or 2 teaspoons of crushed fresh, berries in 1 cup of boiling water for 5 to 10 minutes. Strain, and enjoy.

Labrador Tea

(Ledum latifolium or *L. groenlandicum)*

Other names for this plant are Continental Tea, Swamp Tea, Marsh Tea, Bog Tea, Hudson's Bay Tea, and Moth Herb. During the Revolutionary War, this herb was a popular substitute for China tea. Native to Canada and Greenland, where it grows profusely (hence one botanical name, *groenlandicum*), it can also be found in cold, moist places in the northern areas of the United States, Europe, and Asia. Eskimos and the Indians of eastern Canada used this tea extensively, as did explorers, trappers, and settlers who found imported teas hard to come by. An untidy-looking shrub, Labrador tea is similar in appearance to a straggly rhododendron. Its tea stimulates the nerves, and is believed to alleviate the pains of rheumatism, gout, and arthritis.

PLANT: Perennial. Rust-colored woolly branches bear aromatic, alternate, folded-back, leathery leaves that are green on top, rust-colored and downy underneath. Clusters of scented white flowers appear on the stem ends from May to July.

HEIGHT: 1 to 3 feet.

SOIL: Moist, peat-like.

EXPOSURE: Partial shade.

PROPAGATION: By root divisions taken in mid-autumn, or, less successfully, by seeds.

CARE: Labrador tea is hard to cultivate unless you have a properly cold, damp, exposed site in which to grow it.

PART USED FOR TEA: Leaves gathered throughout the year, except when the plant is flowering. Flowers.

TASTE: Delicate, fragrant. Similar to China tea.

CAUTION: More than 1 or 2 cups of this tea can cause drowsiness and possible poisoning.

How to brew

FLOWERS, BY INFUSION: Steep 1 teaspoon of dried flowers, or 2 teaspoons of fresh flowers, in 1 cup of boiling water.

LEAVES, BY DECOCTION: Crush 1 tablespoon of dried leaves, and add to cup of boiling water. Cover and simmer for 5 to 7 minutes.

Lavender

(Lavandula vera, L. spica, and other species)

The name of this popular purple flower comes from the Latin word *lavare*, meaning "to wash." The ancient Greeks and Romans used lavender in their bath water because of its fresh, clean scent. The attractive lavender flowers are also used in potpourris, sachets, and flower arrangements. The bitter but aromatic leaves are used as seasoning in southern European cooking. As a medicinal plant, lavender is believed to help cure insomnia, nervousness, heart palpitations, and halitosis. It is also used to alleviate flatulence, fainting, and dizziness. Originally native to the Mediterranean, the lavender shrub is cultivated throughout the United States and Europe.

PLANT: Perennial, hardy to 0°F (− 18°C), except *Lavandula dentata* (French lavender), which is hardy only to 15°F (− 9°C). Woody, upright stems have gray, narrow leaves up to 2 inches long, with smooth margins. Lavender-colored flowers rise above the plant in short, clustered spears or on branched flower stalks, depending on the variety. Flowering time is from July to September.

HEIGHT: 1½ to 3 feet.

SOIL: Dry, well-drained, chalky. Not too rich.

EXPOSURE: Full sun.

PROPAGATION: Seeds, difficult to get started, will germinate in 2 to 3 weeks if kept moist and shaded. Also cuttings.

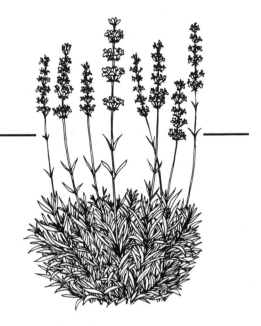

CARE: Space plants 3 feet apart, to avoid fungus diseases caused by inadequate ventilation. Prune when blooming ends in late autumn. Keep ground fairly dry in winter to avoid injury.

PART USED FOR TEA: Flowers. Pick when blossoms are at their prime, and strip them from their stems.

TASTE: Cooling, sweetly aromatic, exotic flavor.

How to brew

BY INFUSION: 1 teaspoon of dried blossoms, or 3 teaspoons of fresh blossoms, to 1 cup of boiling water. Steep to taste.

Lemon Verbena

(Aloysia triphylla, formerly *Lippia citriodora)*

Also called Verbena, Lemon-scented Verbena, Verveine Citronella, and Herb Louisa, Lemon Verbena is native to Peru and Chile—the Spanish call it *Yerba Luisa*—but it was introduced to England and North America by the Spanish during the eighteenth century. In France, it is popularly served as *tisane de verveine.* Verbena's essential oils are considered beneficial as a mild sedative and cooling balm that will help drive away fever. Verbena is also believed to aid digestion.

PLANT: Tender perennial. This is a pot plant in cold-weather climates, where it must be winter-protected. A highly scented deciduous shrub, it bears narrow, lance-shaped, yellow-green leaves—usually in sets of three—on light-colored, woody stems. In August, filmy spikes of tiny white or pale lilac flowers appear.

HEIGHT: To 6 feet under ideal conditions.

SOIL: Light, well-drained soil.

EXPOSURE: Full sun.

PROPAGATION: Seed formation is infrequent, so propagation from cuttings is preferred. Mature plants tend to wilt temporarily after cuttings are made. Once rooted, cuttings are easy to grow and reach maturity in one season. Roots can also be divided in spring.

CARE: Space mature plants about 2 feet apart. Bring lemon verbena indoors before the first frost. Once it is inside, feed

it well-rotted compost or manure regularly, and mist its leaves with tepid water. If it maintains its leaves, they will probably turn darker green. However, don't despair if all leaves drop off, and the plant appears dead. Cut it back in February, and in spring it will come to life again with luxuriant new foliage.

PART USED FOR TEA: Leaves, preferably gathered when the plant is blooming.

TASTE: Warm, lemony. Often added to black *Thea sinensis* teas, and also combines nicely with alfalfa.

How to brew

BY INFUSION: Put 1 teaspoon of dried verbena leaves and tops, or 3 teaspoons of fresh herb, in 1 covered cup of boiling water. Steep for 15 minutes. Strain. Flavor with honey if you like. Good hot or iced.

Licorice *(Glycyrrhiza glabra)*

Other names for this plant are Licorice Root, Black Sugar,
Sweet Licorice, and Sweet Wood. The botanical name
comes from the Greek *glukus* ("sweet") and *rhiza* ("root").
It is said that chewing on licorice root instead of candy has
helped many people to stop smoking without gaining weight;
licorice contains no sugar. Babies have been given a hard
(but not fibrous) piece of washed root to help them cut
teeth. Licorice is found on dry, stony land; it grows wild in
southern and central Europe and parts of Asia. Spain is the
principal exporter of stick licorice. In Arabia, finely powdered
root is used to dry up discharging parts of the skin, to dry
blisters, and to absorb all kinds of watery fluids. Licorice tea
is also a favored remedy for bronchial and stomach problems
—coughs, mucous congestion, and peptic ulcers—as well as
for bladder and kidney ailments.

PLANT: Tender perennial. The 3- to 4-inch flexible and
fibrous taproot is wrinkled and brown on the outside, and
bright yellow inside, with reddish filament roots. The stem
bears alternate leaves with three to seven pairs of dark green
leaflets. Yellowish or purplish flowers appear from June to
August.

HEIGHT: 1 to 3 feet.

SOIL: Deep, sandy, crumbly, well-cultivated. It must be
stone-free so the taproots can grow straight, even though
licorice likes to grow in stony areas.

EXPOSURE: Direct sun.

PROPAGATION: By stem or root cuttings. The root pieces, 3 or 4 inches in length including buds, are red filament roots taken from the plant in March or April.

CARE: Cut shoots or canes to soil level each year in November. By the third autumn, the main root will be mature and can be harvested.

PART USED FOR TEA: Root.

TASTE: Sweet, anise-like. Thirst-quenching.

How to brew

BY INFUSION OR DECOCTION: Use 1 teaspoon crushed or powdered rootstock to 1 cup of boiling water. Steep, or simmer to taste. Serve hot or cold. Added to other herbal teas, licorice will sweeten the brew naturally.

Linden *(Tilia europaea* and other species)*

Linden, also called Lime, European Linden, European Lime Tree, Basswood, and Winged Flowers, is one of the best-known and loved herbs for tea. The tree is found wild in forests and on mountain slopes in Europe. Now cultivated in North America as well as Europe, it is popularly used for lining streets and driveways because of its uniformity. The tea is considered useful in treating colds, influenza, and sore throats. It is also used to relieve mild bladder and kidney problems. Linden tea is said to be good for the skin, helping to keep freckles and wrinkles from appearing. It is also supposed to stimulate hair growth, calm the nerves, and promote sleep.

PLANT: Perennial. This deciduous tree's branches, which spread out at the bottom, bear bright green, 4- to 7-inch, heart-shaped leaves that are coarsely double-toothed. An abundance of small, fragrant, white-to-yellow flowers appears in June and July, attracting bees who make a fine honey from the blossoms. The pea-sized seeds that come after the flowers are often called "monkey nuts."

HEIGHT: 50 to 100 feet.

SOIL: Rich, well-drained, moist.

EXPOSURE: Full sun.

PROPAGATION: By seeds sown during the third lunar phase. They require 2 years to germinate. Also by layering or cuttings, either of which is much quicker.

CARE: Be sure to space trees with consideration for their final size. These trees are easy to grow and are among the few that tolerate the smoke and fumes of the city. However, young trees do need staking and shaping, and if you have transplanted one, be sure to keep it well watered until it is established. Older trees need only corrective pruning.

PART USED FOR TEA: Flowers, which should be gathered when they smell strongly of honey. Once the scent fades, they are too old to use.

TASTE: Similar to chamomile, with a sweet, warm, apple-like taste. Highly aromatic.

How to brew

BY INFUSION: Steep 2 teaspoons of fresh flowers in 1 cup of boiling water for up to 10 minutes. Or use 1 teaspoon of dried flowers.

Marigold
(*Tagetes* species, also *Calendula officinalis*)

This common plant has been called many other names: Calendula, Golden Flower of Mary, Marybud, Gold, Summer's Bride, Sun's Bride, Solsequia, Holygold, and Pot Marigold. The plain marigold or French marigold (*Tagetes* species) is the flower we see in such abundance of variety in hot sunny gardens throughout the United States, while the pot marigold or calendula is a simpler flower which thrives in cool weather. According to legend, this was the flower favored and worn by the Virgin Mary. This marigold of old was a single flower, probably pale yellow. Today hybridists have produced a fantastic range of double-flowered and multi-colored varieties, particularly of the plain marigold. In Brittany, it is believed that a girl who walks barefoot over marigolds will learn the secret language of the birds. Gypsies believe marigolds to be one of the ingredients necessary to see fairies. Marigold tea is rich in phosphorus and vitamin C. It is astringent and induces perspiration. Many believed it to be useful in treating gastrointestinal problems—ulcers, stomach cramps, and colitis—and to bring down fever, prevent vomiting, and heal boils and abcesses.

PLANT: Annual. A branched stem supports unstalked pale to deep green leaves that have widely spaced teeth. Large yellow or orange flowers appear on the terminal stems from June to October. In the *Tagetes* varieties, particularly, both the leaves and flowers give off a bitter, aromatic scent that repels many insects. A chemical produced by the roots repels

nematodes. These qualities make the marigold a favorite border plant around vegetable gardens.

HEIGHT: From 6 inches to 3 feet, depending on variety.

SOIL: Not too rich or moist.

EXPOSURE: Full sun.

PROPAGATION: By seeds sown in early spring during the first or second lunar phase. For a head start, marigolds can be planted in flats indoors; they transplant to the outdoors easily, once danger of frost has passed. Seeds germinate in about 10 days.

CARE: Space or thin plants to about 1 foot apart; crowded seedlings don't flower as well; nor do they make shapely plants. In areas where rabbits eat the foliage, dust the plants with dried blood powder to repel them.

PART USED FOR TEA: Flowers, gathered in the morning after the dew is off. Petals can be used alone for a more delicate tea.

TASTE: Slightly bitter and saffron-like. Petal tea is not as bitter. Sweeten with honey to taste.

How to brew

BY INFUSION: 2 teaspoons of dried flowers or petals, or 4 teaspoons of fresh herb, to each cup of boiling water. Steep for 5 to 10 minutes. The tea is bright yellow.

Marjoram *(Origanum marjorana)*

Marjoram is also called Oregano, Sweet Marjoram, Knotted Marjoram, and Garden Marjoram. It grows wild in the Mediterranean area and in Asia. Greek legend has it that marjoram's sweet scent comes from the touch of the goddess Aphrodite, who first cultivated the flower. As a symbol of happiness, marjoram was formed into garlands to crown brides and bridegrooms. It was also planted on graves to ensure eternal bliss for the departed. And, in the Middle Ages, marjoram was considered a magic charm against witchcraft. Closely related to true marjoram (oregano, *Origanum vulgare*), sweet marjoram (*O. marjorana*) is more delicately flavored. Its camphor-like and tannic properties are believed helpful for gastritis and for children's colic.

PLANT: Perennial, hardy to 15°F (− 9°C), cultivated as a biennial in colder climates where it sometimes winterkills. The square, downy stem has wiry, side branches covered with short-stemmed, small, elliptical, velvety, green-gray leaves. Clusters of pale red or white flowers appear on spikes at the ends of the branches from July to September.

HEIGHT: 1 to 2 feet.

SOIL: Moist, alkaline, light or medium-rich soil.

EXPOSURE: Sun, but sheltered.

PROPAGATION: By seeds sown outdoors in spring during the third lunar phase. Slow to germinate. Also by root divisions

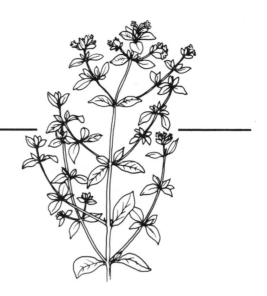

and cuttings in spring. Marjoram is inclined to sprawl and layer itself.

CARE: Space plants 10 to 12 inches apart. Keep seedlings in shade until they are well started. All varieties are slow growing, so cultivate and weed frequently until they are established.

PART USED FOR TEA: Leaves.

TASTE: Sweet, warm, mellow. A flavor that resembles a blend of thyme, rosemary, and sage.

How to brew

BY INFUSION: 2 teaspoons of fresh herb, or 1 teaspoon of dried herb, in 1 cup of boiling water. Steep to taste.

Meadowsweet (*Filipendula ulmaria*)

Also called Lace-makers-herb, Steeplebush, Bridewort, Dollof, Meadsweet, Meadow Queen, Pride of the Meadow, and Meadowwort, Meadowsweet is found wild in damp woods and fens, and on wet rock ledges and river banks, in Asia and Europe. This sweet-scented flower was the favorite of Queen Elizabeth I, who had it scattered over the floors of her private apartment. In Britain, it was also a custom to strew houses with the herb for wedding festivals. Herbalist John Gerard believed this practice wise, saying, "for the smell thereof makes the heart merrie and joyful and delighteth the senses." However, because the perfume of meadowsweet is so heavy, it was believed in other countries that the herb had soporific powers associated with death, and it was considered unlucky to bring meadowsweet into the house. The herb has been used to treat diarrhea and colic. Because it contains salicylic acid, it is said to be a remedy for influenza, respiratory tract problems, gout, rheumatism, fever, and arthritis. It is also recommended for dropsy and bladder and kidney ailments.

PLANT: Perennial. Its creeping root sends up a reddish, angular stem. Large three- to five-lobed, serrated terminal leaflets are slightly hairy underneath. Small yellowish or white flowers appear in dense clusters from June to September.

HEIGHT: 5 to 6 feet.

SOIL: Rich, moist.

EXPOSURE: Partial shade.

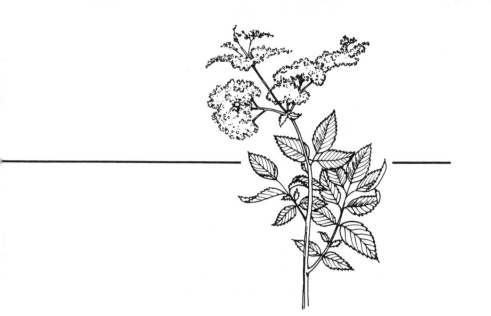

PROPAGATION: Seeds planted during the third or fourth lunar phase. Root cuttings are also easy to obtain, since the rootstock creeps through the wet swampy ground, adds a new piece each year, and sends shoots upward.

CARE: Space mature plants 10 to 15 inches apart. Keep moist.

PART USED FOR TEA: Young leaves gathered before flowerbuds appear. Also flowers and roots.

TASTE: Sweet and delicate, very aromatic.

How to brew

LEAVES OR FLOWERS, BY INFUSION: Place 2 tablespoons of the fresh leaves or flowers, or 1 tablespoon of dried herb, in 1 cup of boiling water. Steep to taste.

ROOTS, BY DECOCTION: Boil 2 tablespoons of dried, crushed rootstock in 1 cup of water. Or soak the dried rootstock in 1 cup of cold water for 6 hours, bring it to a boil, and steep for 1 or 2 minutes.

Mint *(Mentha* species)

There are about thirty varieties of mint found in temperate climates throughout most of the world. These include spearmint, peppermint, orange mint, apple mint, and pineapple mint. Each species is characterized by its soothing, aromatic, refreshing, and distinctive odor and taste, and each has its own degree of bite. Peppermint, for example, is one of the strongest, and the aroma of its crushed leaves symbolized hospitality in ancient Greek and Roman homes. According to Greek mythology, the nymph Minthe was discovered in the arms of Pluto by his wife, Persephone, who crushed the little creature savagely under her foot. Pluto then metamorphosed Minthe into a sweet-smelling plant. Ancient Hebrews covered their synagogue floors with mint leaves, and athletes perfumed their bodies with the leaves to give them power. Mint teas are believed to relieve cramps, coughs, poor digestion, nausea, heartburn, and abdominal pains, as well as headaches, vomiting, and other ailments attributed to nerves.

PLANT: All are perennials, hardy from 5° to -20°F, depending on the variety. Square, branching stems bear opposite oblong, serrated or scalloped dark leaves. The stems are topped by leafless spikes of whitish, violet, red-lilac, or purple flowers that grow densely and bloom from July to September.

HEIGHT: From 18 inches to 4 feet, depending on species.

SOIL: Moist, rich.

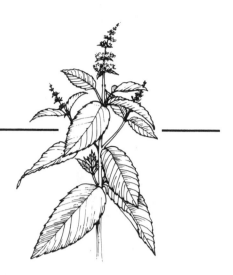

Exposure: Partial shade.

Propagation: Seeds or new shoots in spring during the third lunar phase. Root division in fall. Runners and shoots are easier ways to propagate.

Care: Space from 10 to 15 inches apart, depending on variety. Unless you want seeds, keep mint cut back to improve its growth. Keep weeded. Every 3 or 4 years, renew beds by chopping up the tangled mass of roots with a sharp-edged tool. Water well, cover with a thin layer of enriched soil, and new plants will soon appear.

Part used for tea: Leaves.

Taste: Clean, refreshing, delicately fruity. Aromatic.

How to brew

By infusion: 1 teaspoon of dried leaves, or 3 teaspoons of crushed fresh leaves, in 1 cup of boiling water. Steep to taste. Mint is a popular addition to less tasty herbal teas—alfalfa, for example. All the mint teas are good either hot or cold.

Mugwort (Artemisia vulgaris)

Of Mugwort, whose other names are Felon Herb, Sailor's Tobacco, Smotherwood, Apple-pie, and Old Uncle Harry, John Gerard's *Herball* of 1597 says, "The traveler or wayfaring man that hath mugwort tied about him feeleth no weariness at all." The Pilgrims believed this, too, and it was said that a man who kept mugwort leaves inside his shoes could walk forty miles in a day. Greek legend has it the centaur Chiron taught the goddess of hunting and the moon the uses of mugwort, and she was so pleased with the herb that she gave it her name—Artemis. A strong tea made from the flowers and top leaves is thought to dissolve gallstones, regulate the menstrual cycle, and promote appetite and digestion—all because of mugwort's beneficial effect on bile production.

PLANT: Perennial. This plant has a firm, downy, grooved, brown stem, with alternate, coarsely toothed, green leaves, which are white and downy underneath. Small greenish-yellow to red-brown flowers appear on spikes from July to October.

HEIGHT: 2 to 5 feet.

SOIL: Any moist soil. This plant is considered a weed and can be found in ditches, in waste places, or along roadsides and fences throughout Europe, Asia, and the Americas.

EXPOSURE: Full sun.

PROPAGATION: Seeds planted during the third lunar phase. Also root division; mugwort's creeping roots cause it to spread quickly.

CARE: Place plants 2 feet apart. However, mugwort's reputation as a weed is well deserved, and you'll want to give it plenty of space—perhaps grow it as a large shrub, for example—if you dare to introduce it into your garden. Each year, the circle of roots increases, and it is necessary to cut away many roots and seedlings to keep the plant from getting out of control.

PART USED FOR TEA: Flowers, leaves. Some people brew a root decoction as well.

TASTE: Tangy, refreshing. It was a favorite in England before Oriental tea was introduced.

CAUTION: Drinking more than 1 or 2 cups can lead to symptoms of poisoning.

How to brew

BY INFUSION: 1 teaspoon of dried leaves or flowers, or 3 teaspoons of fresh herb, covered with 1 cup of boiling water. Steep to taste.

Mullein *(Verbascum thapsus)*

Pronounced to rhyme with "sullen," this popular plant has about thirty common names—including Great Mullein, Lady's Foxglove, Velvet Plant, Shepherd's Herb, Old Man's Flannel, Jupiter's Staff, Aaron's Rod, Candlewick, Jacob's Staff, and Witch's Candle—possibly because its towering height, sometimes 8 or 9 feet, makes it hard to ignore. General Agrippa, who served under Caesar Augustus, wrote that the overpowering fragrance of the plant was a deterrent to demons. Early Greeks and Romans dipped flowerheads of the dried stalks in tallow and used them as torches. The tea is considered beneficial for pulmonary disturbances—coughs, asthma, bronchitis, and hay fever. It is also used for sedation and pain relief and alleviation of cramps and gastrointestinal catarrh.

PLANT: A hardy biennial. The tall, stout, single stalk bears 10- to 16-inch, alternate, felt-like, light green leaves. These diminish in size toward the top of the plant, which is crowned by a spike of five-petaled yellow flowers from June to September.

HEIGHT: To 9 feet.

SOIL: Poor, dry.

EXPOSURE: Full sun.

PROPAGATION: By seed sown in spring or fall during the third or fourth lunar phase. Self-sows freely.

CARE: Place plants 3 feet apart. Cut the seedheads in fall unless you want the ground matted with seedlings the following spring.

PART USED FOR TEA: Flowers, leaves.

TASTE: Tea from the flowers is sweet; from the leaves, slightly bitter. Both are highly aromatic.

How to brew

BY INFUSION: Steep 1 teaspoon of dried, or 3 teaspoons of fresh crushed leaves or flowers in 1 cup of boiling water. Be sure to strain this tea well in order to eliminate the fine hairs that cover the plant. Sweeten to taste.

Nettle *(Urtica dioica)*

This plant is also called Common Nettle, Stinging Nettle, Great Stinging Nettle, Indian Spinach, Bad Man's Playthings, and Hoky-Poky. Native to the Northern Hemisphere, it is now found all over the world in waste places and roadsides. In Scandinavian mythology, nettles were sacred to the god Thor, so families threw these plants on the fire during thunderstorms to keep their homes from being destroyed by his lightning. Despite the hazards involved in harvesting it, the rich iron, protein, and vitamin content of the nettle makes the effort worthwhile. The tea is believed to stimulate the digestive system and increase lactation in nursing mothers. Its astringent qualities are said to relieve urinary disorders, rheumatic problems, and colds.

PLANT: Perennial. Nettle's stout stem is densely covered with stinging hairs that contain a venom of formic acid. Serrated, opposite, gray-green leaves are heart shaped and downy underneath. Small, greenish flowers appear in branched clusters from July to September.

HEIGHT: 1 to 8 feet.

SOIL: Rich, moist, full of organic matter.

EXPOSURE: Sun.

PROPAGATION: Seeds planted during the third lunar phase, or new shoots taken in spring.

PART USED FOR TEA: Young leaves, dried.

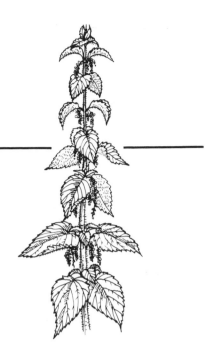

TASTE: Bland, but good with a little mint or other sweetener. The tea is light green.

CAUTION: When handling or harvesting nettle plants, be sure to wear gloves in order to prevent severe stinging, itching, and blistering where the plant touches the skin. Once the greens are cooked or dried they lose their poisonous quality, but never use old leaves uncooked, for they induce symptoms of poisoning and can cause kidney damage.

How to brew

BY INFUSION: Use 2 teaspoons of dried, crumbled nettle leaves per cup of water. Steep 5 to 10 minutes.

New Jersey Tea *(Ceanothus americanus)*

Also called Liberty Tea, Redroot, Jersey Tea, Mountain-sweet, Walpole Tea, and Wild Snowball, this plant is the source of a good caffeine-free tea that tastes like *Thea sinensis*. New Jersey tea is commonly found in dry, sandy, or gravelly soil in woods and thickets ranging from Maine southward to Florida and Texas. After the Boston Tea Party and during the American Revolution, it was one of the teas favored by settlers and soldiers who were boycotting China teas because of the prohibitive taxes the British had placed on them. The tea is believed to relieve chest problems —bronchitis, whooping cough, consumption, and asthma. It is also used as a gargle to alleviate throat and mouth irritations.

PLANT: Hardy perennial; a deciduous shrub. The large root is covered with brownish or reddish bark, and it is red inside. Several upright stems rise from the root cluster. They have alternate, egg-shaped, finely serrated leaves that are dull green on top and finely hairy underneath. On about the first of June, dense groups of small white flowers appear on the ends of the branches. From then until August, this beautiful blooming shrub attracts a wide variety of bees and butterflies.

HEIGHT: To 3 feet.

SOIL: Poor, dry, well-drained.

EXPOSURE: Sun.

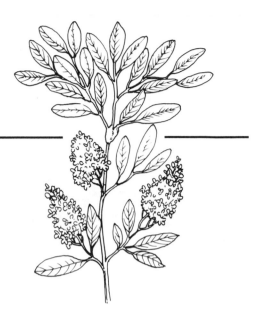

PROPAGATION: By cuttings taken in summer and placed in moist, sandy soil in a cold-frame propagating bed. Also by seeds planted during the third lunar phase, layering, or root division (from side shoots).

CARE: Place plants 4 feet apart. Prune in late winter or early spring, cutting branches back severely, close to the base, and removing unwanted shoots from the previous year's growth.

PART USED FOR TEA: Leaves.

TASTE: Similar to Oriental teas made from *Thea sinensis*.

How to brew

BY INFUSION: Steep 1 teaspoon of dried leaves, or 1 tablespoon of crushed fresh leaves, in 1 cup of boiling water. The dried leaves give more of the Oriental tea flavor. Cream and sugar improve the taste.

Oregano *(Origanum vulgare)*

Oregano is also called Wild Marjoram, Wintersweet, Mountain Mint, and Winter Marjoram. *Origanum* is thought to be the old Greek name for the plant, and means "delight of the mountains." Closely related to marjoram, there is confusion as to which of the two is actually the "real" oregano. Old herbals don't offer much help; they tend to refer to all species of the genus as "organy." Native to the Mediterranean regions, oregano is cultivated in the United States, Mexico, and Europe. It is believed to calm upset stomachs, headaches, indigestion, and other nervous complaints, and it has an ancient reputation as an antidote to narcotic poisoning, convulsions, and dropsy.

PLANT: Perennial, hardy to − 30°F (− 34°C). The rounded, green leaves are opposite from one another on square, purplish stems that rise from creeping roots. The leaves are often larger and coarser and have a darker color than those of sweet marjoram. Purplish-pink blossoms appear at the ends of the stems from July to October.

HEIGHT: 2 to 2½ feet.

SOIL: Average, well-drained, limy.

EXPOSURE: Full sun.

PROPAGATION: Seeds, cuttings, root divisions. Plant seeds in spring or fall during the third lunar phase. Cuttings are easy to root, or new plants can be started by layering. Easier yet,

"instant plants" can be obtained by root division in early spring, since the creeping roots run rampant and are often invasive.

CARE: Space 1½ to 2 feet apart. Keep plants cut back to encourage bushiness and thick foliage. Start new plants from old ones about every 3 years, when the old ones become woody.

PART USED FOR TEA: Leaves.

TASTE: Similar to marjoram, but more intense and stronger in taste and aroma.

How to brew

BY INFUSION: 1 teaspoon dried leaves, or 3 of fresh crushed leaves, steeped to taste in 1 cup of boiling water.

Parsley *(Petroselinum crispum)*

This widespread herb is also called Curly French Parsley, Carum, Rock Parsley, and Common Parsley. It is said that garlands of parsley were worn at Greek and Roman banquets to absorb the fumes of wine and to help prevent intoxication. Rich in chlorophyll content, parsley was also eaten after dining to remove onion and garlic odors, a use that is still popular today. Originally native to southeastern Europe, parsley is now cultivated all over the world. One folk legend connects parsley with death—probably because parsley garlands were given as prizes for Greek and Roman public funeral games that honored the deaths of important people. This ominous association continued into the Middle Ages, when it was believed parsley's wickedness could be overcome if the herb was sown on Good Friday under a rising moon. The tea is believed beneficial in the treatment of asthma, coughs, dropsy, menstrual difficulties, and urinary disorders.

PLANT: Biennial, usually cultivated as an annual. Tufted, finely cut, bright green leaves with serrated or toothed edges rise from a taproot much like a thin carrot; the plant comes from the same family. Greenish-yellow or white flowers appear from June to August of the second year, followed by egg-shaped, grayish-brown seeds.

HEIGHT: 6 to 12 inches.

SOIL: Moist, fairly rich.

EXPOSURE: Shade or partial sun.

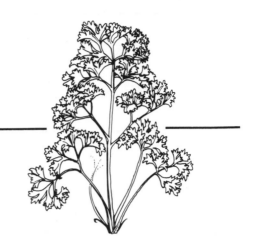

PROPAGATION: Seeds. Germination is slow and uncertain; folk legend has it that the seeds go to the Devil and back several times before they sprout. Germination is hastened if seeds are soaked in warm water for 24 hours before planting.

CARE: Thin seedlings 6 to 8 inches apart. Keep plants well trimmed to encourage bushiness. It's supposed to be unlucky to transplant parsley from an old garden into a new one, but this may be because the taproot of parsley just doesn't transplant well.

PART USED FOR TEA: Leaves harvested before the plants flower.

TASTE: Refreshing, with a cooling taste like that of fresh parsley. Rich in vitamins A, B, C, and K.

How to brew

BY INFUSION: 1 teaspoon of dried, or 3 teaspoons of fresh crushed leaves with 1 cup of water that has stopped boiling. Steep for 20 minutes. Don't boil the fresh leaves.

Pennyroyal (Mentha pulegium)

Other names for this herb are English Pennyroyal and Pudding Grass. A member of the mint family, this more popular species of pennyroyal (there is an American annual version, *Hedeoma pulegioides*, commonly called squawmint) seems to have the power to repel fleas, mosquitoes, and other insects when it is rubbed on the skin. Linnaeus considered this power when he named the plant; *pulex* is the Latin word for "flea." The herb's odor and medicinal virtues come from pulegium, a powerfully aromatic essential oil. Despite its name, English pennyroyal is native to the Near East, though it is now cultivated throughout Europe and North America. Old English herbals say it helps dispel flatulence, produce perspiration, and promote menstruation. It is also believed to relieve spasms and stimulate digestion.

PLANT: Hardy perennial. Creeping roots send up many stems covered with deep green, hairy, oval leaves about ½ inch long. Tiny lilac-colored flowers appear in whorls from June to October. Pennyroyal makes a good ground cover in moist soils.

HEIGHT: Stems up to 14 inches long hug the ground and rise from 4 to 7 inches.

SOIL: Clay, moist soil.

EXPOSURE: Sun or partial shade.

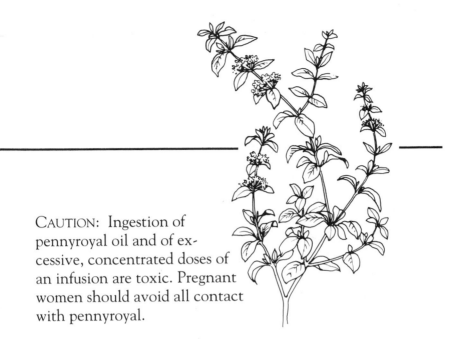

CAUTION: Ingestion of pennyroyal oil and of excessive, concentrated doses of an infusion are toxic. Pregnant women should avoid all contact with pennyroyal.

PROPAGATION: Seeds sown in spring or fall during the third lunar phase. Also stem cuttings. Tiny, rooted stems can be reset in spring or fall.

CARE: Space mature plants from 5 to 6 inches apart. Keep trimmed to prevent straggly stems. Brought indoors, pennyroyal makes a good, aromatic, trailing houseplant.

PART USED FOR TEA: Tops and leaves (before flowering).

TASTE: Strongly minty, sweet, aromatic. The tea has an amber color.

How to brew

BY INFUSION: 1 teaspoon of dried pennyroyal tops and leaves, or 3 teaspoons if using fresh herb, in 1 covered cup of boiling water. Strain, and flavor with honey if desired. Good in combination with other mint teas.

Raspberry *(Rubus strigosus* or *R. idaeus)*

This shrubby plant, which is also called Wild Red Raspberry, is native to the region from Newfoundland to Manitoba, and is found southward as far as New Mexico in the west and North Carolina in the east. Historically, tea from raspberry leaves was given to pregnant women because fragrine, an active substance found in the foliage, affects the female organs of reproduction, especially the muscles of the pelvic region and uterus. Raspberry-leaf tea was also believed to relieve morning sickness and ease childbirth. The red edible fruit found on wild plants is smaller than that from cultivated plants, but just as tasty.

PLANT: Biennial. A durable root sends up thorned, prickly canes, with clusters of irregular, oval, saw-toothed, green leaflets that are whitish and downy underneath. White or greenish-white ½-inch flowers appear in spring or summer of the second year, followed by crimson fruits made up of many tiny plump kernels. Each kernel contains an edible seed. The ripened fruit is juicy and tasty. It appears from July to September.

HEIGHT: To 7 feet.

SOIL: Deep, loamy, well-drained. Moist. Less desirable soils will yield smaller and fewer berries and less luxuriant foliage.

EXPOSURE: Full sun.

PROPAGATION: Seeds, planted during the third or fourth lunar phase, or, more reliably, suckers taken from plants in spring before second-year growth begins.

CARE: Set suckers or seedlings 3 to 4 feet apart, with 6 to 8 feet between rows. Cut back transplanted plants to 12 inches, and set them 3 inches deeper than they were formerly growing to protect the roots from drought. Prune canes back to a height of 3½ to 4 feet before growth begins in spring.

PART USED FOR TEA: Leaves.

TASTE: Astringent, soothing, fruity, and aromatic.

CAUTION: Because of their effect on the female reproductive system, the leaves have acquired the reputation of being aphrodisiac. The tea should be taken in moderation.

How to brew

BY INFUSION: 1 teaspoon of dried leaves, or 3 teaspoons of fresh leaves, to each cup of boiling water. Steep to taste. Can be sweetened with sugar or honey.

Rose (*Rosa* species)

There are more than 10,000 varieties of the rose—the flower of love—because this showy, aromatic, flowering herb has long been the favorite of hybridizers wherever it is grown. Sweet-smelling herbal tea can be made from the petals and rose hips of most varieties. Red rose petals are considered best for petal tea, and the most sought after rose hips come from wild varieties found on sandy beaches, roadsides, waste places, and fields throughout the temperate zones. Legend has it that all roses were white until Aphrodite pricked her foot on a rose thorn, coloring the flower with her blood. The Persian philosopher Zarathustra claimed the rose hip was mother of all nutritious fruits. Hips are noted for their high concentrations of vitamins A, B, E, K, P, and especially C—a cup of rose hips is said to contain as much vitamin C as 150 oranges. Flower tea is believed to fortify the heart and brain and to relieve female ailments, stomach disorders, and catarrh. The genus name *Rosa* comes from the Greek word *rodon*, which means "red."

PLANT: Perennial or tender perennial, depending on the variety. Roses have thorned, erect stems bearing toothed, alternate leaves. Wild flowers are usually single with five petals in shades of white or red, but cultivated varieties can be double- and multi-petaled and come in a wide range of colors. Blossoms are followed by the smooth red or orange hips (fruits).

HEIGHT: Several inches to several feet, depending on the variety.

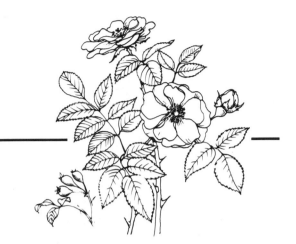

Soil: Most roses require a firm, well-enriched, and well-drained soil.

Exposure: Full sun.

Propagation: Wild varieties can be grown from seeds planted during the third lunar phase. Hybridized varieties require either cuttings or graftings to rootstocks of stronger varieties.

Care: Spacing, pruning, and care depend on the variety and the climate where grown. Consult a book on rose culture to determine what you need.

Part used for tea: Petals gathered before the flower unfolds or hips gathered in early autumn.

Taste: Hips—fruity, aromatic, pleasant tasting. Petals —delicate, exotic, fragrant, like sipping a cupful of flowers.

How to brew

By infusion: 1 teaspoon dried, or 2 teaspoons fresh petals for each cup of boiling water. Steep to taste. Or grind dried hips into powder, and use 1 teaspoon per cup of boiling water. Steep for about 5 minutes, and add a little honey. Both teas are good hot or cold.

Rosemary *(Rosmarinus officinalis)*

Rosemary is also called Dew of the Sea and Mary's Mantle. The symbol of friendship and remembrance, this evergreen shrub is said to bring luck and prevent witchcraft. It originated in the Mediterranean and is widely cultivated. Legend has it that rosemary flowers were white until the Virgin Mary hung her blue cloak over a rosemary bush; from that time on, they were blue. It is said the generic name derives from the Latin *ros,* "dew," and *marinus,* "of the sea." Early herbalists believed wearing a sprig of rosemary could cure nervous ailments and restore youth, and the fragrant tea was thought to relieve flatulence, stimulate the heart, induce sleep, and alleviate headaches. Its rich scent makes it a favorite companion plant in vegetable gardens where it controls cabbage moths, bean beetles, carrot flies, and malaria mosquitoes.

PLANT: Tender perennial. A piny-looking, slow-growing bush, rosemary's many scaly branches are covered with opposite, dark green, narrow, needle-like leaves, which are ashy-white underneath. Pale blue, lavender, or white flowers —resembling tiny orchids—grow on stems that rise above the plant. They bloom during April and May—later in cooler climates.

HEIGHT: 3 to 6 feet.

SOIL: Light, warm, dry, well-drained soil with plenty of lime content.

EXPOSURE: Full sun or partial shade, in a sheltered spot.

182

PROPAGATION: Seeds planted in spring or fall during the third lunar phase. They are slow to germinate—they take 3 weeks or so—and the resulting plants will take 3 years to bloom. Quicker are stem cuttings or 4- to 6-inch root cuttings from new wood or healthy end tips. These root easily when placed in sand, vermiculite, or water.

CARE: Space mature plants 3 feet apart. In cool climates, rosemary must be protected with heavy mulch or brought indoors in winter. The roots are tender and mustn't freeze. Rosemary can be grown as a pot plant. The shrub will grow quickly if it is given lime and fertilizer several times a season.

PART USED FOR TEA: Leaves, flowers.

TASTE: Piny and aromatic, like a fine incense. Good in combination with tansy.

How to brew

FLOWERS, BY INFUSION: 1 teaspoon of dried herb, or 3 tea-spoons of fresh herb, to each cup of boiling water. Steep to taste.

LEAVES, BY INFUSION (VERY STRONG): ½ teaspoon of dried or fresh herb for each cup of boiling water. Good with a little lemon or honey.

Sage *(Salvia officinalis)*

Also called Garden Sage and Purple Sage, this fragrant herb is an ancient symbol of wisdom. It grows wild in southern Europe and the Mediterranean, and is widely cultivated. Sage comes in 700 varieties, including pineapple sage, lavender sage, and others. A member of the mint family, its generic name comes from the Latin *salvia,* meaning "health." Sage is rich in a hydrocarbon known as salvene, as well as in other essential oils. It is astringent, aromatic, stimulating, and bitter. Early herbalists believed sage to be of value in calming nerves, alleviating nervous headaches, and soothing sore throats. It has long been reputed to retard aging, enhance memory, and prevent hands from trembling and eyes from dimming. An ancient Latin proverb translates, "How can a man die when sage grows in his garden?"

PLANT: Hardy perennial. Sage's strongly branched root produces square, hairy stems. Gray-green, 1- to 2-inch, opposite leaves are shaped like elongated ovals and have a coarse surface covered with small bumps. Purple, blue, or white flowers appear on tall spikes in June and July. Placed near the vegetable garden, sage controls cabbage moths, carrot flies, and ticks.

HEIGHT: 2 to 3 feet.

SOIL: Dry, well-drained, sandy or limy soil.

EXPOSURE: Full sun or partial shade.

PROPAGATION: Seeds planted in spring during the third lunar phase. Cuttings. Layering. Root division. Sage also self-sows freely.

CARE: Space plants 18 inches apart. Cut back stems after blooming, and fertilize if you cut the leaves frequently. Overwatering can cause mildew. Renew plants every 3 or 4 years, when they become woody.

PART USED FOR TEA: Leaves.

TASTE: Aromatic, camphor-like, heartening, faintly bitter.

How to brew

BY INFUSION: Cover 1 teaspoon of dried or fresh chopped leaves and tops with 1 cup of boiling water. Steep for 10 minutes. Strain. Sweeten with honey.

Sarsaparilla (*Aralia nudicaulis*)

Also called American Sarsaparilla, Wild Ginseng, Wild
Sarsaparilla, and Wild Spikenard, *Aralia nudicaulis* is a native
American plant. Pronounced "sassparilla" or "sarsparilla," it
was used by the Indians to make a soothing, perspiration-
inducing tea that was believed to alleviate rheumatism, gout,
and skin diseases. The herb thrives in the moist, shaded
forests of southern British Columbia and northeastern
Washington. American sarsaparilla tea is thought to
promote healthy tissue growth for internal and external ulcers
and wounds. Some people used to believe the tea would cure
syphilis. A South American cousin, *Smilax ornato*, is the
evergreen vine used to make the sarsaparilla drink that was
so popular in the late nineteenth century.

PLANT: A tender, deciduous perennial. The long, yellow
taproot is similar to that of ginseng. A single stem branches
into three parts, each having five 2- to 5-inch, finely
toothed, lance-shaped leaves. The flowering stalk that comes
from the root is overshadowed by the leaf stalk. Clusters of
greenish flowers, which bloom from June to August, are
followed by whitish berries that become purple or almost
black when they mature.

HEIGHT: 8 to 12 inches high.

SOIL: Moist, loose, well-drained.

EXPOSURE: Partial shade or shade.

PROPAGATION: Seeds sown as soon as they are ripe. Or, if
that's not possible, they can be mixed with slightly damp

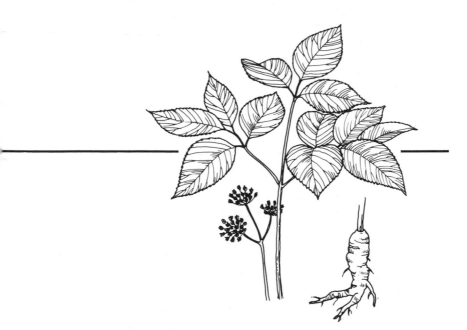

peat moss and stored in plastic bags for 3 to 5 months before being sown. Also by root cuttings of 1 to 1½ inches, placed in sandy, moist soil in a propagating tray that is bottom heated. Be sure that the part of the cutting that was nearest the stem is placed pointing upward in the soil. Also by division of the long horizontal roots in spring.

CARE: This herb grows freely and thrives well with routine management. It is best adapted for semi-wild and informal plantings.

PART USED FOR TEA: The root, dug in autumn.

TASTE: A bitter licorice flavor. Refreshing, fragrant. The tea has a reddish-brown color.

How to brew

BY INFUSION: Stir 2 teaspoons of ground fresh root, or 1 teaspoon of dried crushed or powdered root, into 1 cup of boiling water. Steep to taste. Sweeten with honey or sugar, if desired. Good hot or cold.

Sassafras (Sassafras variifolium or S. albidum)

Other names for this plant are Ague Tree, Cinnamon Wood, Saxifras, and Smelling Stick. A member of the laurel family, the sassafras is native to North American woods. It was used by the Indians long before the first white settlers appeared, and it was one of the first exports from America. When the Spaniards returned from their 1512 voyage to Florida, they brought back news of sassafras, and the Spanish doctor Monardes wrote of it as a medicine and tea as early as 1569. In the past, it was thought infusion of sassafras bark created a "blood purifier," causing perspiration and urination. It was also believed to aid in the treatment of gout, arthritis, rheumatism, and dysentery.

PLANT: Perennial shrub or tree. The stem is covered with thick, rough, reddish-brown bark. The alternate leaves are downy on the underside and may appear in three forms—one simple, one mitten-like, one three-lobed—on one twig. Small, yellowish-green flower clusters bloom from April to June before the leaves appear, followed by pea-sized, yellow-green berries, each of which contains a single seed. The tree attracts the beautiful tiger-swallowtail butterfly, which lays her eggs on the leaves.

HEIGHT: From 15 feet in the North to as tall as 100 feet in the South.

SOIL: Dry or moist sandy loam.

EXPOSURE: Sun or partial shade.

PROPAGATION: By seeds, planted during the third or fourth lunar phase, or stem cuttings.

CARE: Keep soil well drained, and prune the young herb frequently until it is trained. When it is mature, prune only as required for shape. Suckers tend to pop up if roots are cut in cultivating. They should be removed when they appear. This tree has fine autumn coloration.

PART USED FOR TEA: Bark of the root; leaves.

TASTE: Root-beer flavored.

CAUTION: The major chemical constituent of the aromatic oil in the sassafras root bark is safrole, which has been known to cause liver cancer in rats. Despite the continued popularity of sassafras tea, those who drink it should be aware that, until further research has been conducted on the effects of safrole on humans, they may be doing so at their own risk.

How to brew

BY INFUSION: 1 teaspoon of root bark in 1 cup of boiling water. Or 1 teaspoon of dried, or 3 teaspoons of fresh crushed leaves steeped in 1 cup of boiling water. Steep to taste in either case. Good with sugar and cream, hot or cold.

Savory *(Satureja* species)

There are several varieties of savory (sometimes called Bean Herb or Bohnenkraut), including Summer Savory (*S. hortensis*), Winter Savory (*S. montana*), and Yerba Buena (*S. douglasii*). Savory was believed to be a favorite of satyrs because of its peppery taste. Winter and summer savory are the two favorite varieties, and, of these, summer savory is more popular because it has a stronger flavor. Both, however, are deeply aromatic, because they contain caracol, a volatile oil. Savory is a popular condiment for less easily digestible foods such as cucumbers, turnips, and parsnips. The ancient Greeks called savory *isope*, and many wonder whether Old Testament references to hyssop were actually to savory. The tea is believed a remedy for diarrhea, asthma, colic, and digestive disturbances. In 1653, one herbalist, Nicholas Culpeper, recommended it to reduce deafness.

PLANT: Summer savory: annual; winter savory: perennial. Summer savory has a bushy, hairy stem that divides above the ground, and it has dark green, wide, ½-inch-long, needle-shaped leaves. Light pink to violet flowers appear in bunches from July to October, followed by nut-shaped, dark brown or black seeds. Winter savory is a hardy, low-growing shrub, woodier and more bristly than summer savory. It flowers a month earlier than summer savory, and its blossoms are white or pale lavender.

HEIGHT: Summer savory: to 12 inches; winter savory: from 6 to 16 inches.

Soil: Summer savory: rich, dry; winter savory: poor, dry, well-drained, chalky.

Exposure: Full sun for both varieties.

Propagation: Seeds or root division. Summer savory seeds germinate easily. Winter savory seeds have slow, uncertain germination, so the herb is usually reproduced by spring cuttings, side shoots, or layering.

Care: Place summer savory plants 6 inches apart; winter savory plants, 1 foot apart. Summer savory is believed to control bean beetles. Keep both varieties weed free, and hill the plants slightly to keep them upright.

Part used for tea: Leaves gathered before the plant blooms.

Taste: Tangy, marjoram-like.

How to brew

By infusion: 1 teaspoon dried, or 3 teaspoons of crushed fresh leaves to each cup of boiling water. Steep to taste.

Speedwell *(Veronica officinalis)*

Speedwell is also called Veronica, Common Speedwell, Gypsy Weed, Fluellin, Thé de l'Europe, Groundhele, Paul's Betony, and Low Speedwell. This plant is supposedly named for St. Veronica. When she wiped the face of Jesus with her veil as he walked the road to Calvary, it is said an impression of his thorn-crowned head appeared on the scarf and on the flowers she was wearing. The plant is established in dry meadows, woods, and fields in the eastern United States as far south as North Carolina and Tennessee. In Europe, where it is native, speedwell has a reputation for being a universal healer, but in other areas it is best known as a remedy for respiratory problems and stomach ailments. The tea is used to ease migraine headaches and as a gargle for mouth and throat sores. It is also used as a tonic to cure coughs, catarrh, and skin diseases. Speedwell is used in the manufacture of vermouth.

PLANT: Perennial. Speedwell's stems are almost prostrate, turning up only toward the ends. Its opposite, soft, hairy, grayish-green leaves have finely toothed margins. Bright blue flower clusters appear from May to August, followed by hairy capsules containing the seeds.

HEIGHT: Stems grow to about 16 inches, but because they creep, the plant rises only from 3 to 10 inches. It makes a good ground cover.

SOIL: Dry, almost any kind.

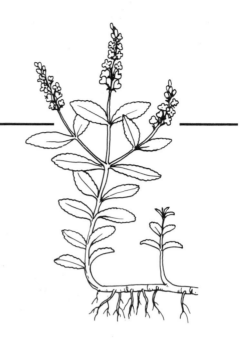

EXPOSURE: Sun, partial shade, shade.

PROPAGATION: By seeds sown during the third lunar phase or by root division.

CARE: Space mature plants 1 foot apart. The plant grows almost anywhere, and it is useful in rock gardens or flower borders.

PART USED FOR TEA: Leaves or whole herb.

TASTE: Bitter, tangy. It was once a universal substitute for China tea.

How to brew

BY INFUSION: Cover 4 teaspoons of the flowering herb, or 2 teaspoons of the dried herb, with 1 cup of boiling water. Steep to taste.

Strawberry (Fragaria vesca)

Other names for this fruit-bearing plant are Wild Strawberry, Hautboy, Wood Strawberry, Woodman's Delight, and Mountain Strawberry. It is said that this plant is the symbol of foresight. In ancient times, people thought the wild strawberry had powers against demons, but today we think of it primarily for its abundant alkali and vitamin C content. The Okanagon Indians of the Pacific Northwest used dried, pulverized leaves to promote healing of the navel of newborn babies. Linnaeus wrote that he cured his gout with fresh wild strawberries. It is believed a tea made from the leaves relieves anemia, lack of appetite, and undue sweating, and prevents miscarriage and menstrual irregularities. It is also thought to relieve diarrhea and jaundice.

PLANT: Perennial. Several stems rise from the root, each bearing three fan-shaped, sharp-toothed, dark green leaves. Small, white, rose-form flowers with five petals and prominent yellow centers appear in clusters during May and June, followed by the seedy, pea-sized, juicy red fruits.

HEIGHT: About 8 inches.

SOIL: Well-drained, rich, moist.

EXPOSURE: Full sun.

PROPAGATION: By seeds or berries planted during the third lunar phase in spring or fall. Or by runners—an easy method because they root themselves or can be rooted by layering.

CARE: Place plants about 8 inches apart. Keep well weeded.
The tiny, extra-sweet berries are delicious but so small that
many must be picked to satisfy even the daintiest appetite.
Our large, cultivated strawberry varieties were developed
from this European plant, hybridized with strawberries from
North America and Chile.

PART USED FOR TEA: Leaves.

TASTE: Cooling, strawberry flavor. Good in combination
with woodruff.

How to brew

BY INFUSION: Cover 3 teaspoons of crushed fresh leaves, or 1
teaspoon of dried leaves, with 1 cup of boiling water. Steep
for about 5 minutes. The fruits also form the basis of a
refreshing hot or cold summer drink. Crush 1 tablespoonful
of berries in a cup, and add boiling water.

Tansy *(Tanacetum vulgare)*

This herb is also called Stinking Willie, Traveller's Rest, Buttons, Alecost, Wild Agrimony, Goose Grass, Parsley Fern, and Hindheal. Tansy's botanical name comes from *athanasia*, the Greek word for "immortality," and it is one of the bitter herbs the Jews were ordered to eat at Passover. Puddings and cakes made with tansy were also traditionally eaten to celebrate the end of Lent, and the herb was used by the ancients for embalming. Tansy grows wild all over Europe and the United States, and it contains tannin, resin, thujone (a chemical component of sage), and tanacetin, which give it its own taste. Herbalists used it to expel worms from the intestines, produce perspiration, and promote menstrual discharge.

PLANT: Perennial. Hardy to − 30°F (− 34°C). Much-divided, rich green leaves grow alternately on the purplish-brown stem. Clusters of small, button-like, bright yellow flowers appear from July to September. The seed is a hard, one-seeded fruit.

HEIGHT: 3 feet.

SOIL: Any well-drained chalky soil.

EXPOSURE: Full sun.

PROPAGATION: By seeds planted in spring or fall during the third lunar phase. Or by root division. Self-sows freely.

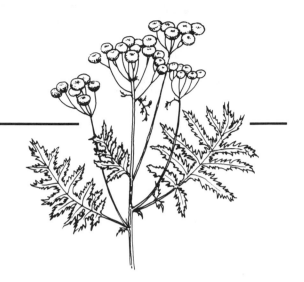

CARE: Space plants 4 feet apart. Stake against wind and rain if they are in an unprotected spot. Cut off dead stems in fall; the plant will reappear in spring. Don't allow tansy to become too wet, and thin each year to prevent rapid spreading.

PART USED FOR TEA: Leaves and tops.

TASTE: Bitter, lemony. Can be sweetened with honey. Good in combination with rosemary.

CAUTION: In moderate doses the herb has a mild, tonic effect, but in larger quantities—more than 1 or 2 cups—it can be violently irritating and narcotic. Use with caution —tansy can be poisonous!

How to brew

BY INFUSION: 1 teaspoon of dried, or 2 teaspoons of fresh crushed leaves and tops. Cover with 1 cup of boiling water, and steep for a short period only. Serve tansy tea weak, and drink it in moderation.

Thyme *(Thymus vulgaris)*

Pronounced "time," this popular herb is also called Common Thyme, Broad-leaf English Thyme, Black Thyme, Garden Thyme, Shepherd's Thyme, and Mother Thyme. Kipling wrote of the "wind-bit thyme that smells of dawn in Paradise," but he was hardly the first to sing its praises. Thyme was a favorite of the early Greeks and Romans, and the Roman poet Virgil praised honey drawn from thyme, saying the mountains "Hymettis in Greece and Hybla in Sicily were so famous for bees and honey because there grew such a store of thyme." Christian tradition holds that thyme was among the herbs in the manger bed where the Christ child lay. Herbalists considered thyme a strong antiseptic and thought it could calm the nerves, alleviate indigestion, and clear the mucous membranes. It was also thought to overcome shyness—the generic name *Thymus* is believed to be a derivation of the Greek *thymon*, which means "courage."

PLANT: Perennial, hardy to −20°F (−29°C). There are many species, but common thyme *(T. vulgaris)* is the one usually used for tea or seasoning. It is semi-woody, shrubby, and covered with ¼-inch-long, oval, gray-green leaves. Small clusters of bluish-purple flowers appear at the ends of the stems from May to September. Seeds follow.

HEIGHT: 6 to 12 inches.

SOIL: Dry, light, limy.

EXPOSURE: Full sun.

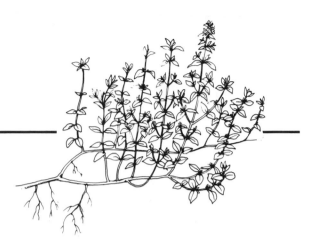

PROPAGATION: By seeds planted in spring and fall during the third lunar phase. They take about 2 weeks to germinate if kept at exactly 70°F (27°C), which isn't easy to do. Also by stem cuttings, layering, or division of roots, which is much easier.

CARE: Space plants about 1½ feet apart. Thyme can't tolerate dampness, so be sure the site you choose is well drained. Rock gardens are an ideal spot. Thyme is called the "poor man's herb" because it needs no added nutrients aside from those in the soil it's planted in. Do keep it weeded, though. This herb is often companion-planted near cabbage because its scent helps control cabbage worms. Replace the plant with a younger one every 3 or 4 years, when it gets woody.

PART USED FOR TEA: Leaves.

TASTE: Pungent, spicy.

How to brew

BY INFUSION: 1 teaspoon dried leaves and tops, or 3 teaspoons of fresh crushed herb, in 1 covered cup of boiling water. Steep for 10 minutes. Strain and flavor with honey. A pinch of rosemary in the brew gives added zest.

Valerian (Valeriana officinalis)

Valerian is also called Garden Heliotrope, All-Heal, Setwall, Capon's Tail, Phu, Vandal Root, and St. George's Herb. While the flowers of this herb are pleasantly fragrant, the rest of the plant is not. Herbalists Galen and Dioscorides aptly called it "*phu*," because of its pungent, unpleasant aroma. Cats and rats, however, delight in valerian's odor. It is suggested this herb was the secret power the legendary Pied Piper of Hamelin used to rid the town of its rats. Herbalists have recommended this tranquilizing herb for all nerve-related ailments—migraine headaches, hysteria, vertigo, anxiety, insomnia, hypochondria, and nervous convulsions. The name *valerian* is believed to come from the Latin *valere*, meaning "to be powerful" or "of well-being." Native to Europe and Asia, it is represented nearly throughout the world by related species.

PLANT: Perennial. The short, tuberous root sends up a round, hollow, grooved stem with light green leaves that grow in pairs and that are further divided into eight to ten pairs of narrow leaflets. In June, white, pink, or lavender-blue flowers appear in clusters at the ends of the stems. Their strong scent is like that of heliotrope. Because of its high phosphorus content, valerian attracts earthworms, making it a favorite plant to place near the vegetable garden.

HEIGHT: 4 feet.

SOIL: Somewhat heavy, moist, rich.

EXPOSURE: Full sun or partial shade.

PROPAGATION: By seeds planted in spring or fall during the third or fourth lunar phase. Just press them into the soil, don't cover. They are slow to germinate. Also by root (rhizome) division in spring or fall.

CARE: Space plants about 2 feet apart. Because valerian's creeping roots spread quickly, divide the plant every other year. Enrich the soil with manure before replanting.

PART USED FOR TEA: Root, harvested in fall.

TASTE: Soothing, strongly scented.

CAUTION: The sedative qualities of this tea make it a time-honored antidote for insomnia when taken in small doses. However, if more than 1 or 2 cups are drunk daily, in large or frequent doses, the herb is dangerous, producing reverse effects—nervous agitation, vertigo, muscle spasms, even hallucinations. It should be used sparingly.

How to brew

BY INFUSION: ½ teaspoon of ground or powdered dried valerian root in 1 cup of boiling water. Steep for 10 minutes or to taste. Strain. Flavor with honey or an aromatic spice —mace is a good one.

Wintergreen *(Gaultheria procumbens)*

Also called Partridge Berry, Periwinkle, Spiceberry, Checkerberry, Deerberry, Teaberry, Boxberry, Wax Cluster, Canada Tea, and Mountain Tea, this small, creeping evergreen is a native of southern Canada and the United States. The leaves contain oil of wintergreen and are sharply astringent and aromatic, making them a favorite flavoring agent; wintergreen is a common ingredient in home-made root beer. The common names "deerberry" and "partridge berry" were coined because deer and partridge also know a good thing and love to eat the plant's berries. It's said wintergreen tea is good for many kinds of aches and pains, from headaches to rheumatism. It is also used to alleviate colds and fever.

PLANT: Perennial. An evergreen shrub. Wintergreen's stems creep on or beneath the surface of the ground, rooting themselves and sending up erect branches. Young leaves are lighter green, often with a reddish tinge. Single, nodding, bell-shaped, white flowers grow near the tops of the branches from May to September, followed by scarlet berries, which are about ⅓ inch in diameter.

HEIGHT: 2 to 6 inches.

SOIL: Acid, sandy, rich, and well-drained.

EXPOSURE: Shade or partial shade.

PROPAGATION: By seeds planted during spring or fall during the third lunar phase. Also by division of the rooted stems in fall or spring. The herb can be layered as well.

CARE: Wintergreen makes a good ground cover. Its ideal location is in pine woods, and it is a favored wild garden plant. It is difficult to establish plants taken from the woods; nursery-grown plants take better. Plant them on a shady slope, and mulch them with 2 to 4 inches of pine needles.

PART USED FOR TEA: Young leaves.

TASTE: Wintergreen flavor, cooling and refreshing.

How to brew

BY INFUSION: Cover 1 teaspoonful of crushed or chopped leaves with 1 cup of boiling water. Allow to steep for a few minutes to release the maximum amount of oil of wintergreen.

Woodruff *(Asperula odorata)*

Other names for this plant are Sweet Woodruff, Master of the Woods, Moth-herb, Wood-rose, Woodward, Wood Rova, and Muge-de-bois. The fresh, woodsy odor of woodruff, strongest when the plant begins to die away after flowering, has given it many of its common names. For example, the old French name—*muge-de-bois*—means "wood musk." German May wines are steeped in woodruff twigs and owe their fine aroma and taste to the chemical coumarin, in which the herb is rich. In medieval times, woodruff was hung in bunches with roses, box, and lavender on the feast days of St. Peter and St. Barnabas. The herb is supposed to repel insects, which is why it is sometimes called moth-herb. Herbalists believe the tea is a good remedy for kidney and bladder troubles (especially obstructions and stones), liver congestion, and gall-bladder difficulties. It is also recommended in cases of dropsy and insomnia.

PLANT: Hardy perennial. Its deep green, starry whorls of six to eight shiny, lance-shaped leaves surround the erect stem. The plant sends up leaf whorl after leaf whorl, finally topped with a flat-topped flower cluster of small white star-shaped flowers that bloom in May and June.

HEIGHT: 8 to 10 inches.

SOIL: Slightly acid, with high humus content, preferably beech-leaf compost. Moist.

EXPOSURE: Shade.

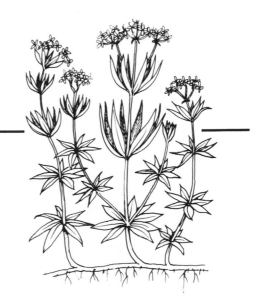

PROPAGATION: By seeds planted in fall during the third lunar phase. Germination takes 200 days, but this method is uncertain. Woodruff can also be propagated by division of the creeping root system once the herb has covered an area of 2 square feet. This is more dependable.

CARE: Space plants 12 inches apart. Weed when necessary. Don't hoe, though, or you'll destroy the spreading root system. Fertilization is unnecessary if the plant is growing in the right soil.

PART USED FOR TEA: Dried leaves.

TASTE: Resembles Darjeeling tea. Mild, sweet, with a woodsy taste. Good in combination with strawberry.

How to brew

BY INFUSION: 1 teaspoon dried leaves in 1 covered cup of boiling water. Steep for 15 minutes. Strain and sweeten to taste with honey.

Yarrow (*Achillea millefolium*)

Yarrow is also called Old Man's Pepper, Knight's Milfoil, Soldier's Woundwort, Nosebleed, Devil's Plaything, Bloodwort, Hemming and Sewing, Staunchweed, Carpenter's Weed, Thousand Seal, and Sanguinary. Yarrow's Latin name, *Achillea millefolium*, derives from Greek mythology: Before the siege of Troy, the centaur Chiron told Achilles of the plant's healing virtues so he could use it on his warriors' battle wounds. *Millefolium* means "a thousand leaves," and refers to yarrow's finely cut foliage. An important first-aid treatment through the centuries, yarrow's astringency is thought to stem the flow of internal and external bleeding. Herbalists also have faith in yarrow tea to induce perspiration, cleanse the system, and cure a bad cold. Straight dried yarrow stems are "thrown" by Chinese fortunetellers before consulting the *I-Ching*—the Book of Changes, an ancient guide to oracular wisdom.

PLANT: Perennial, hardy to − 30°F (− 34°C). The creeping rootstock sends up clumps of grayish-green stems, which branch toward the top and bear alternate, feathery, deeply cut leaves. From June to November, grayish-white, pale lavender, or yellow flowers appear at the stem ends in flat-topped clusters.

HEIGHT: 3 feet.

SOIL: Average or poor. Well-drained. Moderate moisture.

EXPOSURE: Sun or partial shade.

PROPAGATION: Seeds planted indoors in March during the third lunar phase. More commonly, by root division in spring or fall or transplant of self-sown seedlings.

CARE: Place plants 12 inches apart. If they are cut back after the first flowers fade, they may bloom again in fall. Divide clumps every other year.

PART USED FOR TEA: Leaves and/or flowers gathered during summer and fall.

TASTE: Mildly astringent. Somewhat like a mild sage tea. Pale yellow in color.

How to brew

BY INFUSION: 1 teaspoon dried yarrow leaves and flowers, or 1 tablespoon of the fresh herb, in 1 covered cup of boiling water. Steep for about 10 minutes. Strain. Sweeten with honey to taste.

Growing herbal teas

Reference chart

	PLANT TYPE			HEIGHT			
	HARDY PERENNIAL	TENDER PERENNIAL	ANNUAL OR BIENNIAL	UNDER 1 FOOT	1 TO 3 FEET	3 TO 5 FEET	OVER 5 FEET
AGRIMONY	●				●	●	
ALFALFA†	●				●		
ANGELICA†			●		●	●	
ANISE			●		●		
BALM†	●				●	●	
BASIL†			●		●		
BAY*†		●				●	●
BEE BALM	●				●		
BETONY	●				●		
BIRCH	●						●
BLACKBERRY		●				●	●
BORAGE†			●		●		
BURNET†	●				●		
CARAWAY			●		●		
CATNIP*†	●				●		
CHAMOMILE†	●			●			
CHRYSANTHEMUM†	●			●	●	●	

*Special care is required in the preparation of this tea. Consult the compendium for specific instructions.
†This herb may be grown successfully indoors.

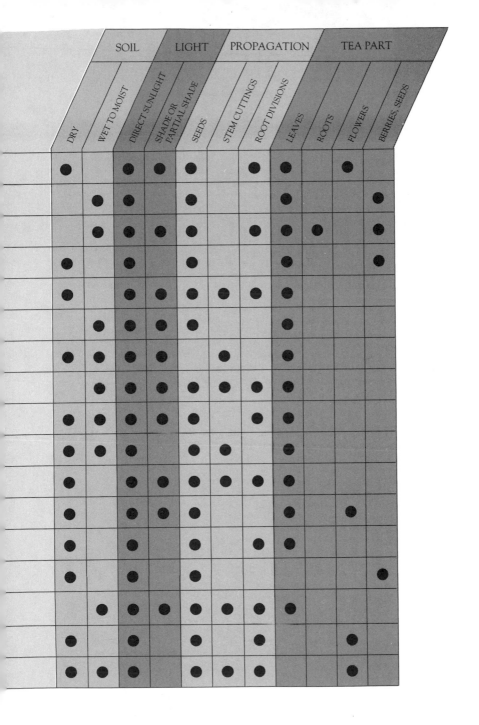

| | SOIL | | LIGHT | | PROPAGATION | | | TEA PART | | | |
	DRY	WET TO MOIST	DIRECT SUNLIGHT	SHADE OR PARTIAL SHADE	SEEDS	STEM CUTTINGS	ROOT DIVISIONS	LEAVES	ROOTS	FLOWERS	BERRIES, SEEDS
	●		●	●	●		●	●		●	
		●	●		●			●			●
		●	●	●	●		●	●	●		●
	●		●		●			●			●
	●		●	●	●	●	●	●			
		●	●	●	●			●			
	●	●	●	●		●		●			
		●	●	●	●	●	●	●			
	●	●	●	●	●		●	●			
	●	●	●		●	●		●			
	●		●		●	●	●	●			
	●		●	●	●			●		●	
	●		●		●		●	●			
	●		●		●			●			●
		●	●	●	●	●	●	●			
	●		●		●		●			●	
	●	●	●		●	●	●			●	

Reference Chart

	PLANT TYPE			HEIGHT			
	Hardy Perennial	Tender Perennial	Annual or Biennial	Under 1 Foot	1 to 3 Feet	3 to 5 Feet	Over 5 Feet
Cicely	●				●		
Clover†	●				●		
Coltsfoot	●			●			
Comfrey *	●				●		
Dandelion†	●			●			
Dill†			●		●		
Elder	●						●
Fennel†	●				●		
Fenugreek			●	●			
Flax*			●	●			
Fraxinella*	●				●		
Geranium†		●			●	●	
Ginseng	●			●			
Goldenrod	●				●	●	
Hawthorn	●					●	●
Hibiscus			●		●	●	●
Hollyhock			●				●
Hop*		●					●

*Special care is required in the preparation of this tea.
Consult the compendium for specific instructions.
†This herb may be grown successfully indoors.

| | SOIL | | LIGHT | | PROPAGATION | | | TEA PART | | | |
	DRY	WET TO MOIST	DIRECT SUNLIGHT	SHADE OR PARTIAL SHADE	SEEDS	STEM CUTTINGS	ROOT DIVISIONS	LEAVES	ROOTS	FLOWERS	BERRIES, SEEDS
		●		●	●		●	●			
		●	●		●					●	
		●	●		●		●			●	
		●	●	●	●		●	●	●		
	●	●	●	●	●			●	●		
	●		●		●			●			●
		●	●	●	●	●	●	●		●	
	●	●	●		●		●	●			●
	●		●		●			●			●
		●	●		●						●
	●		●		●		●	●	●		●
		●	●			●		●			
	●	●		●	●				●		
	●		●	●	●		●	●		●	
		●	●	●	●	●				●	●
		●	●		●					●	
		●	●	●	●					●	
		●	●	●	●	●		●		●	●

	PLANT TYPE			HEIGHT			
	HARDY PERENNIAL	TENDER PERENNIAL	ANNUAL; OR BIENNIAL	UNDER 1 FOOT	1 TO 3 FEET	3 TO 5 FEET	OVER 5 FEET
HOREHOUND†	●				●		
HYSSOP	●				●		
JASMINE†		●				●	●
JUNIPER	●					●	●
LABRADOR TEA*		●			●		
LAVENDER†	●				●		
LEMON VERBENA†		●				●	●
LICORICE		●			●		
LINDEN	●						●
MARIGOLD†			●	●	●		
MARJORAM†		●			●		
MEADOWSWEET	●						●
MINT†	●				●	●	
MUGWORT*		●			●	●	
MULLEIN			●			●	●
NETTLE*	●				●	●	●
NEW JERSEY TEA	●				●		
OREGANO†	●				●		

*Special care is required in the preparation of this tea.
Consult the compendium for specific instructions.
†This herb may be grown successfully indoors.

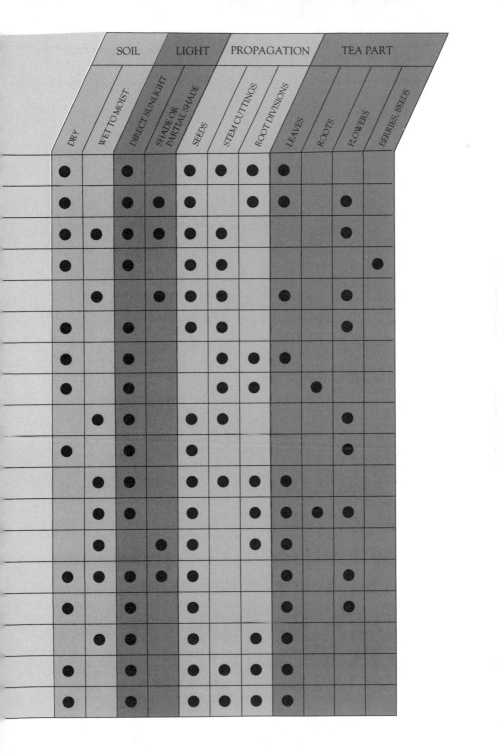

	PLANT TYPE			HEIGHT			
	HARDY PERENNIAL	TENDER PERENNIAL	ANNUAL OR BIENNIAL	UNDER 1 FOOT	1 TO 3 FEET	3 TO 5 FEET	OVER 5 FEET
PARSLEY†			●	●			
PENNYROYAL*†		●			●		
RASPBERRY*			●				●
ROSE		●		●	●	●	●
ROSEMARY†		●			●	●	●
SAGE†	●				●		
SARSAPARILLA		●		●			
SASSAFRAS*	●						●
SAVORY†	●		●	●	●		
SPEEDWELL	●			●			
STRAWBERRY†		●		●			
TANSY*†	●					●	
THYME†	●			●			
VALERIAN*	●				●		
WINTERGREEN†	●			●			
WOODRUFF†	●			●			
YARROW	●				●		

*Special care is required in the preparation of this tea.
 Consult the compendium for specific instructions.
†This herb may be grown successfully indoors.

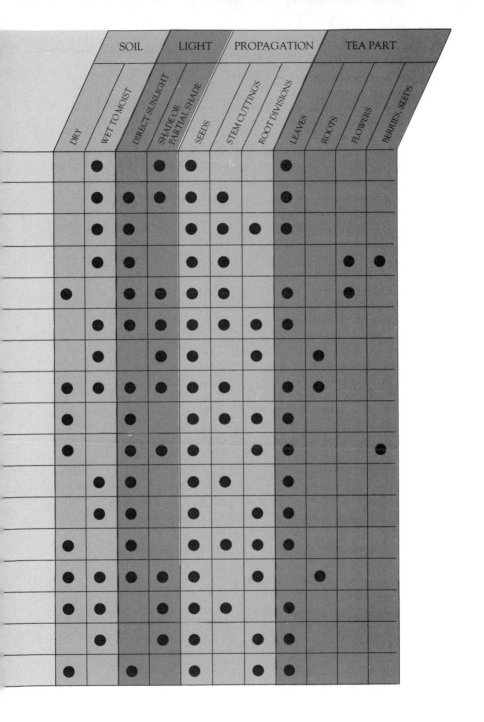

Sources for Seeds and Plants

Your local nursery or garden center is likely to carry a variety of seeds and plants. To order by mail or to obtain product information, consult the companies listed below. This is only a partial listing. *The Complete Guide to Gardening* by Mail is available from The Mailorder Association of Nurseries, Department SCI, 8683 Doves Fly Way, Laurel, MD 20785. Please add $1.00 for postage and handling in the United States, $1.50 for those in Canada.

Another good reference for sources is *The Herb Companion Wishbook and Resource Guide* by Bobbi A. McRae (Interweave Press, 201 East Fourth Street, Loveland, CO 80537).

Many of the suppliers listed below allow visitors to tour their gardens and nurseries. It's wise to check before visiting, though; some are open only during the spring, summer, and fall months.

Abundant Life Seed Foundation
P.O. Box 772
Port Townsend, WA 98368
(360) 385-5660

Bountiful Gardens
18001 Shafer Ranch Road
Willits, CA 95490
(707) 459-6410

W. Atlee Burpee and Company
300 Park Avenue
Warminster, PA 18974
(800) 888-1447

Caprilands Herb Farm
534 Silver Street
Coventry, CT 06238
(860) 742-7244

Carroll Gardens
444 E. Main Street
Westminster, MD 21157
(800) 638-6334

Circle Herb Farm
4548 Hejal Road
East Jordan, MI 49727
(616) 536-2729

Clark's Greenhouse and
Herbal Country
2580 100th Avenue
Box 15B
San Jose, IL 62682
(309) 247-3679

Companion Plants
7247 N. Coolville Ridge Road
Athens, OH 45701
(614) 592-4643

Comstock, Ferre, and Company
P.O. Box 125
Wethersfield, CT 06109
(800) 733-3773

Country Lane Herbs
R.R. 3
Puslinch, ON
Canada N0B 2J0

Cricket Hill Herb Farm
Glen Street
Rowley, MA 01969
(978) 948-2818

Elixir Farm Botanicals
Elixir Farm
Brixey, MO 65618

The Flowery Branch Seed
    Company
Box 1330
Flowery Branch, GA 30542
(770) 536-8380

Fox Hill Farm
444 W. Michigan Avenue
P.O. Box 9
Parma, MI 49269
(517) 531-3179

The Fragrant Path
P.O. Box 328
Fort Calhoun, NE 68023
(402) 468-5782

Gilbertie's Herb Garden
7 Sylvan Avenue
Westport, CT 06880
(203) 227-4175

Glade Valley Nursery
9226 Links Road
Walkersville, MD 21793
(301) 845-8145

Godwin Creek Gardens
P.O. Box 83
Williams, OR 97544

The Gourmet Gardener
8650 College Boulevard
Overland Park, KS 66210
(913) 345-0490

Hartman's Herb Farm
Old Dana Road
Barre, MA 01005
(978) 355-2015

Herbamed Nursery
P.O. Box 209
Bermagui South
Australia NSW 2547

The Herbfarm
32804 Issaquah-Fall City Road
Fall City, WA 98024
(206) 222-7103

Herb Gathering
5742 Kenwood
Kansas City, MO 64110
(816) 523-2653

It's About Thyme
11726 Manchaca Road
Austin, TX 78748
(800) 598-8037

Le Jardin du Gourmet
P.O. Box 75
St. Johnsbury Center, VT 05863
(800) 748-1446

Lily of the Valley Herb Farm
3969 Fox Avenue
Minerva, OH 44657
(330) 862-3920

Krystal Wharf Farms
RD 2 Box 2112
Mansfield, PA 16933
(717) 549-5194

Lewis Mountain Herbs &
Everlastings
2345 Street Route 247
Manchester, OH 45144

Logee's Greenhouses
141 North Street
Danielson, CT 06239
(888) 330-8038

Meadowbrook Herb Garden
Route 138
Wyoming, RI 02898
(800) 569-7603

Merry Gardens
P.O. Box 595
Mechanic Street
Camden, ME 04843
(207) 236-9064

Nichol's Garden Nursery
1190 N. Pacific Highway
Albany, OR 97321
(541) 928-9280

Park Seed Company
Cokesbury Road
Box 31
Greenwood, SC 29647
(800) 845-3369

Prairie Moon Nursery
Route 3 Box 163
Winona, MN 55987
(507) 452-1362

Rasland Farm
Route 1 Box 65
Godwin, NC 28344
(910) 567-2705

Rawlinson Garden Seed
269 College Road
Truro, NS
Canada B2N 2P6

Richters Herbs
357 Highway 47
Goodwood, ON
Canada L01 1A0
(905) 640-6677

The Rosemary House
120 South Market Street
Mechanicsburg, PA 17055
(717) 697-5111

Sandy Mush Herb Nursery
Route 2
Surrett Cove Road
Leicester, NC 28748

Shepherd's Garden Seeds
30 Irene Street
Torrington, CT 06790

St.-John's Herb Garden, Inc.
7711 Hillmeade Road
Bowie, MD 20720
(301) 262-5302

Sunnybrook Farms Nursery
9448 Mayfield Road
Chesterland, OH 44026
(440) 729-7232

Tinmouth Channel Farm
Box 428B, Town Highway 19
Tinmouth, VT 05773
(802) 446-2812

INDEX

bronchitis, 74, 96, 138, 166, 170
catarrh, 76, 106
Burnet, 45, 50, 92–93, 208–9

Caffeine, 13
Calendula officinalis. See Marigold
Camellia thea. See China tea
Camellia sinensis. See China tea
Candy, 74
Caraway (Carum carvi), 52, 94–95, 208–9
   in blends, 61–62
Catarrh, 88, 114, 120, 180
Catnip, 14, 62, 96–97, 208–9
   cultivation, 32, 34, 45
Ceanothus americanus. See New Jersey Tea
Chamomile, 15, 98–99, 208–9
   in blends, 60, 62, 63
   cultivation, 45
Chervil, 49, 51
Chest pain, 128
Chest problems, 120, 134, 170
Chicory, 66
Childbirth, 80
China tea, 9–11, 55
   in herbal blends, 60, 65–66
   substitutes, 60
Chrysanthemum (Chrysanthemum species),
   100–101, 208–9
Cicely, 62, 102–3, 210–11
Clover, 62, 104–5, 210–11
Cloves, 63, 64, 65
Coffee substitute, 66
Colds, 72, 114, 118, 138, 154, 168, 202,
   206
Colic, 74, 76, 96, 116, 158, 160, 190
   flatulent colic, 94, 98
Colitis, 156
Color in the herb garden, 38, 39, 41–42
Coltsfoot, 60, 106–7, 210–11
   propagation of, 34
Comfrey, 108–9, 210–11
Concentrate, for teas, 57
Constipation, 68, 78, 104
Consumption, 140, 170
Convulsions, 172, 200
Coriander, 52, 61–62
Coughs, 72, 102, 104, 106, 120, 138, 140,
   152, 162, 166, 174, 192
   whooping cough, 170

Courage, 90
Cramps, 76, 144, 162, 166
Crataegus species. See Hawthorn

Damping-off disease, 21
Dandelion, 15, 64, 110–11, 210–11
   as a coffee substitute, 66
   indoor cultivation, 45
   wine, 65
Debility, 88
Decoction, 56–57
Dehydrator, 51
Diarrhea, 88, 136, 160, 190, 194
Dictamnus albus. See Fraxinella
Digestion, 80, 94, 108, 134, 120, 150, 162,
   164, 168, 176, 190. See also
   Dyspepsia; Indigestion
   aid to, 70
Disease, in herb plants, 21, 28, 46–47
Dill, 60, 112–13, 210–11
   cultivation of, 19, 28, 45
   harvesting, 50, 52
Diuretic, 144
Dizziness, 148
Dreams, 84
Dropsy, 128, 160, 172, 174, 204
Drug addiction, 70
Drying herbs, 50–53, 54
Dry places, herbs for, 40
Dysentery, 92, 124, 188
Dyspepsia, 76

Earaches, 134
Eczema, 86, 138
Elder, 114–15, 210–11
Elderberry, 58
Elderflowers, 60, 65
Elderflower wine, 65
Elimination, 70
Enema, 96
Enteritis, 78
Eye problems, 142

Fainting, 148
Fennel, 52, 61–62, 116–17, 210–11
   cultivation of, 45
Fenugreek, 60, 118–19, 210–11
Fertilizers, for herbs, 27–28, 46–47

212–13
cultivation, 44, 45
Jaundice, 194
Juniper (*Juniperus communis*), 60, 144–45, 212–13

Kidney problems, 130, 152, 154, 160, 204
stones, 110, 122

Labeling plants, 19–20
Labrador Tea, 060, 146–47, 212–13
Lactation, 74, 78, 90, 94, 116, 118, 168
Laurus nobilis. *See* Bay
Lavender (*Lavandula vera, L. spica*), 60, 64, 148–49, 212–13
cultivation of, 29, 31, 45
Layering, 33–34
Laxative, 102–3
Leaves, 49–52. *See also specific herb*
in blends, 15
brewing of, 56
drying of, 50–52
Ledum latifolium or *L. groenlandicum*. *See* Labrador Tea
Lemon Balm. *See* Balm
Lemon Verbena, 50, 51, 150–51, 212–13
in blends, 60, 61, 62
cultivation of, 29, 44, 45
Licorice, 60, 63, 152–53, 212–13
as a sweetener, 58
Light, 22–23, 45–46
Linden, 154–55, 212–13
Linum usitatissimum. *See* Flax
Lippia citriodora. *See* Lemon Verbena
Liqueurs, 74
Liquor, in blends, 63–64
Liver ailments, 68
Lung problems, 106, 120

Mace, in blends, 64
Marigold, 60, 156–57, 212–13
Marjoram, 60, 62, 158–59, 212–13
cultivation, 19, 45
harvesting, 49, 50
Marrubium vulgare. *See* Horehound
Meadowsweet, 63, 160–61, 212–13
Medicago sativa. *See* Alfalfa
Melancholy, 76, 90
Melissa officinalis. *See* Balm

Memory, 94, 184
Menstruation, 74, 94, 108, 122, 164, 174, 176, 194, 196
Mentha pulegium. *See* Pennyroyal
Mentha species. *See* Mint
Microwave oven drying, 51
Migraine, 76. *See also* Headache
Mint, 50, 60, 65, 162–63, 212–13
cultivation of, 45
Mintale, 66
Moist places, herbs for, 40
Monarda didyma. *See* Bee Balm
Moth repellant, 204
Mound layering, 34
Mouth problems, 170
inflammation, 68, 134
sores, 192
Mucous membranes, 198
congestion, 116, 152
Mugwort, 164–65, 212–13
Mulching, 26–27
Mullein, 60, 166–67, 212–13
Myrrhis odorata. *See* Cicely

Nausea, 74, 82, 162
Nepeta cataria. *See* Catnip
Nerves, 90, 96, 132, 146, 148, 154, 162, 172, 182, 184, 198, 200
Nettle, 168–69, 212–13
New Jersey Tea, 60, 170–71, 212–13
Nightmares, 61

Ocimum basilicum. *See* Basil
Orange mint, 66
Orange peel, 58, 62, 66
Organic gardening, 21
Oregano, 50, 172–73, 212–13
cultivation, 19, 27, 45
propagation of, 29, 34
Origanum marjorana. *See* Marjoram
Origanum vulgare. *See* Oregano
Oswego tea. *See* Bee Balm
Outdoor garden, 18–20, 41
Oven drying, 51

Pain, 202
Painkiller, 84, 166
Panax quinquefolium. *See* Ginseng
Parsley, 174–75, 214–15

cultivation, 27, 45
harvesting, 50, 51
Pelargonium species. *See* Geranium
Pennyroyal, 176–77, 214–15
Peppermint, 61, 62. *See also* Mint
Perennial herbs, 18, 39
Perlite, 30, 31
Perspiration, 114, 128, 156, 176, 186, 188, 196, 206
Petroselinum crispum. *See* Parsley
pH, 17–18, 47
and mulch, 27
Pimpinella anisum. *See* Anise
Planning the herb garden, 18, 26, 38–48
Pleurisy, 172
Poison antidotes, 90, 102, 110, 138, 172
Poterium sanguisorba. *See* Burnet
Potting mix, 20
Pregnancy, 76, 118, 178, 194
Propagation, 29–37
cuttings, 30, 32
layering, 33–34
root division, 34–36
by seed, 29
Pulmonary problems, 138, 140. *See also* Asthma; Bronchial problems; Consumption; Coughs; Lung problems; Respiratory problems; Whooping cough
Punches, herbal, 66

Raspberry, 36–37, 178–79, 214–15
in blends, 63, 65
Respiratory problems, 160, 192
Rheumatic pain, 72, 86, 110, 120, 146, 160, 168, 186, 202
Rock gardens, herbs for, 41
Root cuttings, 32
Root division, 34–36
Roots, 52–53. *See also specific herb*
in blends, 58, 60, 63–64, 66
brewing of, 56–57
Rose (*Rosa* species), 180–81, 214–15
petals, 62
Rose geranium, 65
Rose hips, 61, 62, 63. *See also* Rose
Rosemary (*Rosmarinus officinalis*), 60, 61, 62, 64, 182–83, 214–15
cultivation, 44, 45

harvesting, 50, 51
propagation, 29, 31, 45
Rubus species. *See* Blackberry
Rubus strigosus or *R. idaeus*. *See* Raspberry
Runners, 36–37

Sadness, 76
Sage, 60, 62, 184–85, 214–15
cultivation, 31, 33, 45
Salad burnet. *See* Burnet
Salvia officinalis. *See* Sage
Sambucus nigra. *See* Elder
Sand, 30, 31
Sanguisorba minor. *See* Burnet
Sarsaparilla, 186–87, 214–15
propagation of, 29
Sassafras (*Sassafras variifolium* or *S. albidum*), 14, 63, 188–89, 214–15
Savory (*Satureja* species), 32, 45, 190–91, 214–15
harvesting, 49, 50
Scented geranium, 29, 44–45, 63, 65. *See also* Geranium
Secuda, 14
Sedative, 98, 150, 166
Seedlings, 19, 20, 24–25
Seeds, 52, 61–62. *See also specific herb*
brewing of, 56–57
for planting, 18–20, 22–23, 29
Sexual rejuvenator, 126
Shade, herbs for, 40
Shingles, 138
Shortness of breath, 84
Skim milk, as fertilizer, 28
Skin problems, 86, 154, 186, 192, 194
Sleep, 68, 74, 136, 154, 182
Snakebite, 142
Soil, 16–18, 25, 30–31, 39
for indoor plants, 21, 46–47
Solidago odora. *See* Goldenrod
Sore throats, 128
Spearmint, 60, 61, 62, 64, 66. *See also* Mint
Speedwell, 192–93, 214–15
Stachys officinalis. *See* Betony
Stamina, 70
Stem cuttings, 29–31
Stevia, 14
Stimulants, 102, 110, 114
Stomach problems, 78, 108, 116, 132, 152,